STORIES FROM THE HEART
Teachers and Students Researching
Their Literacy Lives

Richard J. Meyer
University of Nebraska, Lincoln

LAWRENCE ERLBAUM ASSOCIATES, PUBLISHERS
1996   Mahwah, New Jersey

Lawrence Erlbaum Associates, Inc., Publishers
10 Industrial Avenue
Mahwah, New Jersey 07430

Cover design by Gail Silverman

Library of Congress Cataloging-in-Publication Data

Meyer, Richard, J., 1949–
Stories from the heart : teachers and students researching their
literacy lives / Richard J. Meyer.
p. cm.
Includes bibliographical references and index.
ISBN 0-8058-8044-5 (p : alk. paper)
1. Teachers—United States—Biography. 2. Student teachers
—United States—Biography. 3. Storytelling—United States. 4.
Action research in education—United States. I. Title.
LB1775.2.M49 1996
371.11′00973—dc20   95-41474
                                                                            CIP

Books published by Lawrence Erlbaum Associates are printed on acid-free paper, and their bindings are chosen for strength and durability.

Printed in the United States of America
10 9 8 7 6 5 4 3 2

STORIES FROM THE HEART
Teachers and Students Researching
Their Literacy Lives

This book is for *Lillian Florence Meyer* because,
on her lap and in her rocking chair,
she told me the stories, sang me the songs, and chanted the poems
of the past, the present, and the possibilities.

And for the memory of *Robert Meyer*
who worked hard, laughed hard, and
could survive being swamped in a canoe and
come up with his pipe still in his mouth.

And for *Sadie* and *Zoe*
who are helping me create new stories
as our lives wrap around each others'.

And, for *Pat*.

And for *teachers* and *students*
who tell
the stories of their lives.

Contents

Preface

Children and teachers are not disembodied intelligences, not instructing machines and learning machines, but whole human beings tied together in a complex maze of social interconnections. The school is a social world because human beings live in it.
—Waller (1932, p. 13)

This book is for, by, and about teachers and preservice teachers understanding themselves as curious and literate beings, making connections with colleagues, and researching their own literacy and the literacy lives of their students. It is meant to help teachers by acknowledging our successes, our struggles, and our never-ending desire to support children and ourselves in learning. The book is about our stories—the stories that teachers (including preservice teachers) tell of living and learning with children, colleagues, and as part of a school's culture.

We all have stories. We know what it is like to wake up at 3 a.m. and not be able to fall back to sleep. We stare at the ceiling in our dark bedrooms as the faces of students come to mind. We see the faces of those students we are worried about; they shook us out of our restful slumber and now they keep us awake. Or, perhaps we see the faces of children as we relive a classroom success. Our classrooms and our lives are ongoing narratives that deserve telling. This book is for preservice and inservice teachers who are or want to become researchers by being storytellers. I have included some teachers' stories as demonstrations of the types of stories some of us are collecting. The telling of the stories of our lived experiences as teachers helps makes us better teachers, keeps us alive as learners, and helps us understand what is unfolding before our eyes in our classrooms.

The book has six chapters. Chapter 1 demonstrates the power and importance of story in our lives as literate individuals. It includes literacy autobiographies of the author and of preservice and inservice teachers. Readers are encouraged to tell or write or recreate in some way the stories of their literacy lives in order to understand how they learn and teach. Chapter 2 begins the journey into writing the stories of others' literacy lives. Short literacy stories presented in this chapter show how reminiscing, recalling, and reflecting can be important tools for learning and understanding what happens in classrooms. Chapter 3 gives longer stories. The story of Zoe, a kindergarten child, and Robert, a fourth grader, are included in this chapter. Readers learn how stories are framed by what others have written and about trusting our own insights into children's literacy activity. Chapter 4 offers ideas for finding support in our researching endeavors; many support system possibilities are presented. Chapter 5 examines in greater depth the idea of framing stories by using the work of other teachers and researchers. Chapter 6 is for the ever reluctant writer who has read the entire book and still has not written anything.

It's time to tell the stories of our classrooms and our lives as teachers. Our stories are a viable and valid form of research because our stories teach us and teach others when we share them. Telling our stories is a form of liberation. It is one way we claim our classrooms as belonging to us and our students. I hope that even as you read this book you begin to write about your life as a teacher and a learner and that you share the stories you are writing. Perhaps you will also encourage your students to write the stories of their lives. You might coauthor, with your students, the stories of your learning lives overflowing into each others'.

Our stories are our power. Telling them makes us articulate experts about our classrooms. The purpose of this book is to help both preservice and inservice teachers and students as they research their literacy lives, tell their literacy stories, and enrich the social literacy world of schools.

ACKNOWLEDGMENTS

I had a lot of help writing this book. My family missed me many weekends and late nights as I wrote; I thank Pat, Sadie, and Zoe for being understanding of my commitment to writing. Zoe was a very excited and conscientious coresearcher for much of the work presented in chapter 3. Sadie read and commented on sections; Pat read and commented on the first draft.

Many teachers helped to write this book, too. Cindy Brown and Stacy Kuszak contributed literacy autobiographies as part of the work we did together exploring our own and our students' literacy lives one summer. Laura Yohn and Michelle Hempel contributed their literacy autobiographies; Laura's writing is a celebration of a glorious journey. Michelle faced some hard realities in writing her piece; she found out that she is just beginning to understand and come to terms with her literacy life. Kara Osborne and Robert found out much about each other and themselves as they became co-researchers in writing one of the longer stories in chapter 3.

Risa Udell read parts of the manuscript and commented on them. She is a gentle reader and a fine colleague whom I thank for her help. I thank Larry Andrews for his faith in me and for connecting me with an editor with a heart. Naomi Silverman, the editor, was quite supportive, helping me to live with some of the loneliness a writer faces.

Kathy Short was a strong supporter of this work. She read drafts and commented on them, with comments that were supportive, clear, and rich with insight. Thanks, Kathy, for the way you believe in me.

MaryAnn Manning read an earlier draft of this book and offered such encouragement that I think I walked 2 inches off the ground for days after discussing it with her. John Manning, who read pages as MaryAnn finished them, was also quite supportive.

Hanna Fingeret, a good friend and outstanding scholar, has been an important person in the story of my life since we met in elementary school. For 40 years, we have shared our stories, lived adventures, and reflected on our learning and growth.

And I thank all of the children and teachers I know and who know me. Their lives—connecting to my life in seemingly infinite ways—have helped to make this book come about. I look forward to their stories and their books.

—Richard J. Meyer

chapter 1

Our Own Stories

> *Long ago, when I was a young man, my father said to me,*
> *"Norman, you like to write stories?"*
> *And I said, "Yes, I do."*
> *Then he said, "Some day, when you're ready, you might*
> *tell the story of our family. Only then will you understand*
> *what happened and why."*
> —*A River Runs Through It* (Redford & Markey, 1992)

Teachers often rely on stories to 'understand what happened and why.' Sitting in the teachers' lounge at noon or after school, a small group of teachers inevitably gathers to talk about their day or week or semester. If we are fortunate to be among a caring faculty, the teachers listen to each other, offer some advice or information, and then move on to the next person's story. These brief moments can be healing, informative, helpful, nurturing, and, quite often, fleeting.

This book is about stories that teachers tell. It is about cultivating those stories so that we can understand what it is we are learning as we live our lives in our classrooms. It is about writing down our stories because we know that writing shapes thinking (Applebee, 1984). We don't only learn to write; we write to learn. Don Murray and Don Graves have shown us that taking pen in hand, or pencil or keyboard, might begin as an exercise in retelling certain events. But as we learn to show our life to an audience (real or imagined), we also begin to learn about the events we're writing about. In order to write about something, we come to understand parts of it we hadn't thought of before. Even as I write this book, I find my mind moving in many different directions. What shall I write next? How can I move smoothly to what I think comes next? I am often surprised by the answers to these questions because what I actually write is not foreseeable; it changes as it unfolds.

1

Writing is a craft. I like to think of writing that way. I picture a potter at her wheel with a huge lump of spinning clay before her. She wets her hands and places her thumbs on the center part of the clay and caresses it with her fingers. She has a piece in mind, but it also seems that the clay has a piece in mind. They, the clay and the potter, seem to negotiate the piece together. This image comes to me from living with an art educator for 15 years. Yet, it fits writing. I feel more comfortable with writing when I think of it as a craft. The words are my medium. I work with them, and then find that they are working with me. I stop and reread what I have written, just as the potter slows the wheel and leans back to view the spinning piece before her. Her eyes move up and down the piece of clay. My eyes move up and down the piece of writing. The clay and the potter tell a story. The potter moves parts, might even squish the piece and begin again, but each piece teaches. So it is with writing.

A writer must give to his or her piece the same kind of attention that the potter gives to her piece. I must have a relationship with my written piece, with my story. The story, then, moves beyond the actual event that I might want to retell. It takes on a flavor of its own, a uniqueness that is different from what actually happened. If it is a story I choose to recall and retell orally, rather than in writing, it becomes a sort of tape in my mind that I rerun when I want to tell it. It changes subtly each time I retell. Perhaps you have stories like this. It is not uncommon for us to have stories of our lives in a family that change over time. I might tell the story differently to my younger daughter than I would to my best friend. The audience changes the way the story is told. We frame stories to fit the time, the setting, and our relationship with the audience. Madeline Grumet (1991) asked writers to write multiple versions or accounts of stories:

> Multiple accounts splinter the dogmatism of a single tale. If they undermine the authority of the teller, they also free her from being captured by the reflection provided by a single narrative. (p. 72)

But what of one-version writing? Surely we can't change our written stories because they are right before us in black and white. Our stories change each time we read them. Louise Rosenblatt (1938/1978) demonstrated this as she explained reader response theory. Each time we read a story, what we bring to that story changes because of our recent experiences, past experiences, mood, and much more. The nagging questions emerge. Why should teachers bother to write stories of their lives within and beyond their classrooms? Who would read them? What good would they do? How would they help the teacher become a better teacher? Why do we need to explore ourselves through writing? Are stories the way to do this?

Rosenblatt (1938/1978) wrote about her work with children and the stories they read:

The students valued literature as a means of enlarging their knowledge of the world, because through literature they acquired not so much additional *information* as additional *experience*. New understanding is conveyed to them dynamically and personally. Literature provides a *lived-through*, not simply *knowledge about*: not the fact that lovers have died young and fair, but a living-through of *Romeo and Juliet*; not theories about Rome, but a living-through of the conflicts in *Julius Caesar* or the paradoxes of *Caesar and Cleopatra*. In contrast to the historian's generalized and impersonal account of the hardships of the pioneer's life, they share the hardships of Hansa and Beret in Rolvaag's *Giants in the Earth.* (p. 38)

So it is with our own writing about our lives as teachers—indeed, our lives. We move beyond "knowledge about" rather quickly; it is the making sense of the "lived-through" that stories offer us. In their construction and reading, we come to know who we are.

This isn't easy for most of us. Our writing is something we must come to every day. It needs to be part of what we do to nourish and maintain ourselves. Natalie Goldberg (1986) compared writing to

running, the more you do it, the better you get at it. Some days you don't want to run and resist every step of the three miles, but you do it anyway. You practice whether you want to or not. You don't wait around for inspiration and a deep desire to run. It'll never happen, especially if you are out of shape and have been avoiding it. But if you run regularly, you train your mind to cut through or ignore your resistance. You just do it. And in the middle of the run, you love it. When you come to the end, you never want to stop. And you stop, hungry for the next time.

That's how writing is, too. Once you're deep into it, you wonder what took you so long to finally setting down at the task. (p. 11)

Geane Hanson is a colleague and friend of mine. Recently, she studied children's daydreams (Hanson, 1992) and the ways in which those daydreams touch and are touched by children's lives in schools. The children in her study experienced a wide range of teachers. Some were caring. Some were not. Some were structured. Some were not. Some relied on power and control, whereas others constructed classroom life with the children in a way that distributed power and decision making. Although her work focuses on the lives of the children, as a teacher I view her findings about teachers quite informative. Geanne told me, "You are who you teach and you teach who you are."

When Geanne said this to me, I realized that it made sense to write this book. Too many times, I taught children things I was not proud of. On reflection, I found that what the children were doing was rooted in who I was as a teacher. Sometimes this simply meant that they, for example, relied on mathematic algorithms rather than understanding the mathematical concepts I thought I was teaching. In literacy, this meant that they were writing the way I was writing; the way I thought they should write because it was the way I wrote. I was disappointed in them, in the quality of their writing, but looking deeper I found the disappointment rested within me. I was teaching who I was—as a writer, as a mathematician, and as a human.

This book is intended to be a mixture of stories I have lived and continue to live, suggestions of ways to begin writing your own stories, and vehicles for interpreting stories for our growth as teachers. This means that our stories saturate the contexts in which we teach and that understanding our stories helps us make sense of what happens in our classrooms.

Many years ago I was told a story that has 'stuck.' It seems tucked away and arises at just the right moment, I like to think. Two Zen monks are walking down a road together. One is a master and the other is a neophyte, new to the dwelling where this particular order of monks lives. They walk along in silence and eventually arrive at a place in the dirt road that is thick, wet mud. Standing on the same side of the muddy road as the monks is a young beautiful woman. She seems upset that the road is impassibly muddy and there seems to be no way around it.

The older monk asks her if he can help and proceeds to carry the woman through the mud. (I guess Zen monks don't care much about being muddy.) He places her down on the other side of the mud and the two monks continue walking in silence. When they reach their dwelling, the younger monk can no longer contain himself, "I can't believe that you would violate the rules of our order!" he shrieks. "You touched a woman. You carried her."

The older monk looks at the younger and replies, "I put the woman down on the other side of the mud. You are still carrying her" (Zen Buddhism, 1950, p. 41).

So it is with our own stories. We carry them unless they become no longer important. Some of the stories I present in this book are from my many years of teaching. Some reach back to the beginning of my teaching career in 1972. Others are more recent. Because they are the stories I still carry, they are the ones teaching me. They are the stories I believe have something to teach others, too, as I rely on the stories in my teaching of graduate and undergraduate courses at the university. I have also included other teachers' stories in this book; their stories are inspirational and offer demonstrations of other ways of thinking and writing.

Something about our stories runs deep within us, like the river referred to in the quote at the beginning of this chapter. Students in the classes I teach will often recall stories I have told them and use them as springboards to discussions of things happening in their field experiences or thoughts they have in response to their reading. They seem to intuit the power of stories as they start to collect stories of their own.

Stories bind a culture or groups of people. Our teaching stories bind us. The stories of our families bind us. Stories do seem to cross cultural boundaries as a way of teaching, learning, remembering, making sense of things, understanding what happens to us, and even predicting what will happen to us. This book is about the power of stories and their use in helping us to become better teachers. It can start, for me, in only one place. It needs to start with my own story.

MY LITERACY LIFE

Why would I write my own story and how would I go about it? I'd write it because I teach who I am and I want to know who that is and how I got that way. Writing my own story, which tends to be a multitude of stories, helps me make sense of some of the dilemmas I face as a teacher and to resolve some of the tension and contradiction I feel. For example, as a second-grade teacher, I relied on the basal for part of the first year of my primary teaching experience, in spite of the fact that it was not part of my teacher preparation program. That teacher education program, quite progressive for its time, was based in the idea of immersing children in quality children's literature to teach reading. I couldn't do that because I just plain hated to read. And there is the beginning of a story: hating to read. Where did that come from? How did I resolve it? I need to understand that process of resolution. Writing helps me think through to resolution and it changes the resolution, too. Writing makes my thinking more solid and expansive at the same time.

It doesn't make sense that I would hate to read. Still, that is the emotion I recall even as far back as first grade when we sat at the round, red reading table with our noses aimed at our basal readers. The main characters in our books were Tom, Betty, Susan, and their parents and pets. And there was, within me, a deep-rooted pain about all of it. I think some of the pain was that I felt different.

On a typical evening in our very Jewish home near New York City, my father would work late. Many weeks, we saw him only on weekends because he was gone before we rose in the morning and arrived home well after we had gone to sleep. My mother would perform the ritual of getting us to bed. We had those Golden Books with the gold and black tape along the edge of the cover. I cannot remember one single title we had, but I remember the ritual. The three of us, my two sisters (one older and one younger) and I, would squeeze onto my mom's lap in a darkly stained wooden rocking chair. She would read to us.

Then, after the story, she would sing. That's when the rocking would begin. "Shamai Y'Israel, Adonai elohaynue, Adonai echad." We heard the words. Over and over, night after night, we heard songs of our culture. Years later, as a student in Hebrew school, I would learn what these words meant. It didn't matter. These strange words were a musical system of their own. They were part of the physical and psychological bonding that took place between my mother and my sisters and me. Some nights, one or the other of us did not want to be touched by our siblings and would push the others' feet and hands away from ourselves. Other nights, we would flop all over each other, gently rocking and hearing the songs.

This type of literacy learning is visceral. It involves the whole body. In some way, my relationship with my mother was renewed in this process. My relationships with my sisters were complemented. Jim Trelease (1985) discussed the importance of the beat of nursery rhymes; they resemble the first beat a child hears—that of his or her mother's heartbeat within the womb. Trelease wrote that the security of the womb might be linked to the literacy events in a child's life. I love this metaphor because the importance of safety and comfort in learning should never be underestimated. The safety and comfort of the rocking chair are powerful examples of conditions that nurture learning.

During different holiday seasons, different Hebrew songs would be sung. The rocking, the books, our breathing together, our touching—all of it formed the tight bond of who we are as a family. I remember flannel pajamas and teddy bears on that chair. I remember the dark black of my mother's eyes. I remember feeling so peaceful. It was an ideal context in which to learn Hebrew songs, create lasting memories, and invent myself within my culture.

But school was different. Tom and Betty's mother was slim and long. She baked the kinds of cookies I thought could only be found in bags in stores. The tragedies in their lives revolved around their dog hiding or their kites caught in trees. Our tragedies at home had to do with members of the family who were prisoners of war, the anti-Semitism in our community, a cousin dying of multiple sclerosis, and the constant flow of family members who visited us, lived with us, and left us.

Tom and Betty had great days, too. They put on plays and rarely went to school. When they finally did go to school, it was because we were in second grade and *school* and *teacher* were vocabulary words listed at the back of the book. The kids on my street had successes that were different from those of Tom and Betty. We put on plays, but it seemed like getting ready for the play, writing the script, and arguing over who would get which part left the actual performance anticlimactic. Play production was quite complex. Such complexity rarely fit into Tom and Betty's lives.

Tom and Betty lived far from my block. To learn to read from Tom and Betty almost seemed like a kind of betrayal.

Now wait a minute! We're talking about a first-grade boy here. Me. A child of 6, in school, learning to read. Am I about to paint a picture of a failing learner and attribute that failure to the subtle cultural differences between Tom and Betty and me? Is this the story of every school failure that I am trying to portray via my own? No.

My story of learning to read—and I did learn to read in that first-grade classroom—is a story I did not leave at the school building. It's important to me because I am trying to make sense of my literacy life. I am writing my literacy autobiography in order to understand myself, but not simply for self-indulgence or self-aggrandizement. This is my story and, as such, it becomes part of every story that unfolds during the year in my classroom. It is important, almost urgent, that I reflect on who I am and how I got here. Going back to first grade means finding the roots of my own literacy learning and the roots of my literacy teaching.

The thing I remember most about being in school is wanting to be at home. Some days, I would come home and sit in that rocking chair. It wasn't near the television. I would sit and rock and sing, "Shmai Y'Israel. ..." Looking back on these memories, I make sense of them just as Rosenblatt suggested. I make sense of them in light of what I know and understand now. I work at taking the strand that is this memory and follow it as it is woven into my life today.

The recollection of my mom's rocking and reading and becoming enculturated as a Jew came to me when I was reading Herb Kohl's (1991) book, *I Won't Learn From You*, in which he discussed the role of assent in learning. A learner must agree to the conditions of learning in order for learning to take place. Kohl wrote:

> Deciding to actively not-learn something involves closing off part of oneself and limiting one's experience. It can require actively refusing to pay attention, acting dumb, scrambling one's thoughts, and overriding curiosity. The balance of gains and losses resulting from such a turning away from experience is difficult to assess ...
>
> Because not-learning involves willing rejection of some aspect of experience, it can often lead to what appears to be failure. For example, in the case of some youngsters, not-learning to read can be confused with failing to learn to read if the rejection of learning is overlooked as a significant factor. (p. 13)

The memory is important as part of who I am as a reader. I did not fail in school, but I can acknowledge that I was uncomfortable and, at times, not safe. Nancy Meltzoff (1993) reported on a kindergarten classroom in which the rule was "Everyone must feel safe and comfortable." Safety and comfort are important parts of classroom life in the classes I teach at the university and were important when I was teaching young children, too, of course. Writing about these issues means that I make sense of the intuitions upon which my classroom rests. I seem to have a sense about safety and comfort and by writing about them I make those intuitions explicit. This seems to make room for further intuitions and more writing. That is how I am growing as a teacher.

The story I wrote about my mother's singing, my home, and learning to read, is my earliest literacy learning recollection. I "found" it when I was reading Kohl's book. By 'found,' I mean that it rolled forward from somewhere deep in my mind. Perhaps your reading of this story stirred such a memory in you. Now is the time to write it. Consider putting this book down and writing about your recollection. Let your mind wander far back in time.

Picture teachers, fellow students, and classrooms. Picture the ride to school or the walk to school or perhaps the bike ride. Find that salient moment and write about it. Sometimes it appears as a still photo in your mind. Other times it is a video in motion. Perhaps you recall a smell, or the way something felt to your touch. Do you remember the pattern on the walls of your school? Or the famous artists whose work was posted on those walls? The smells of the cafeteria? The tree outside the building, or the bike rack? Can you see the cafeteria workers? Your first classroom? Who were your friends? What did you say to each other? Play? Sing?

My recollection emerged from my relationship with a particular book. In that sense, it may be considered an *intertextual* (Short, 1992) event. One text, a book, brought to mind another text, the text of my memory. The recollection made Kohl's book powerful for me. Teachers like to hear about or read about the lives and experiences of other teachers. Such stories typically result in a string of stories, as in the teachers' lounge described at the beginning of this chapter. These are also intertextual events.

The professional literature on teachers' learning and change supports the importance of teachers' stories. Some groups of teachers are systematically framing their stories within the literature. They are studying a particular philosophy or theory, most notably whole language and reading–writing classrooms, and weaving their stories into that theory or philosophy. Teachers are researchers when they do this. We have always been researchers but we have not typically received the recognition and prestige that researchers seem to gain. But this is changing. Our stories are valued within the larger research community. Many researchers are working at being invited into classrooms to assist teachers in telling their stories.

John Dewey (1904) believed in teachers' stories. He knew that we are pressured by many other facets of education and that if left to study who we are, we will do so with rigor and depth:

> The tendency of educational development to proceed by reaction from one thing to another, to adopt for one year, or for a term of seven years, this or that new study or method of teaching, and then as abruptly to swing over to some new education gospel, is a result which would be impossible if teachers were adequately moved by their own independent intelligence. The willingness of teachers, especially of those occupying administrative positions, to become submerged in the routine detail of their callings, to expend the bulk of their energy upon forms and rules and regulations, and reports and percentages, is another evidence of the absence of intellectual vitality. If teachers were possessed by the spirit of an abiding student of education, this spirit would find some way of breaking through the mesh and coil of circumstance and would find expression for itself. (p. 107)

Reading Dewey was an inspirational part of my graduate education. But how did I reach the point of wanting to read Dewey when I have already disclosed my distaste for reading as a child?

I wrote book reports by copying the flaps on dustjackets and would never choose a book that lacked a jacket for such a project. Reading was not filling some deep need. As my mom's lap grew smaller (or is it that I grew larger?), bicycle adventures took the place of the rocking chair. Coming home from school, I would head out for places unknown. Wednesday afternoons were prime adventure times because Thursday was special trash day. On Thursdays, we were to put out trash that was too large for garbage cans. This included old televisions, radios, washers, dryers, and other appliances. These were the stuff of inventions. On Wednesdays I traveled with a pair of pliers in my pocket so that I could remove important pieces for future inventions. Much like the plays we put on, thinking of and gathering materials for these inventions far exceeded any actual production.

Clearly, I love to play. Riding in my Toyota station wagon on the way to campus, when I see an old television or a discarded baby buggy or stroller, I envision a robot or go-cart. An old lawnmower by the side of the curb at one house and a rusty sprinkler near another set my mind wandering. I think that *play* is the key word. When I speak of writing as a craft, it is because craftspeople seem to be constantly at play. In my first teaching job, I taught in a small rural district. There, I was befriended by the fifth-grade science teacher. Here was a man who could play! He made dulcimers, looms, and garden tools on weekends! He helped me realize that the most powerful scientists are probably the hardest players.

Vygotsky (1978) wrote that a child is a head taller when at play. We, as adults, often marvel at the 2-year-old who plays for hours with cardboard boxes or the 7-year-old who constructs elaborate ramps for marbles or toy cars to run down. *Play* is the link that I found between my life at home and my life in school. When I was at school, I had to do work. This was a job. It was something that needed to be completed so that I could be free from its burden. Home was the zone of play. It was a place where the agenda was mine to choose. Certainly, I had the typical chores, but these didn't consume the time I had to wander and wonder. At school, I was a head shorter.

This all relates to uncovering my love of reading and writing. Typical of many teachers who do not enjoy reading and writing (see Gray & Troy, 1986; Manna & Misherr, 1987; Mour, 1977; Searls, 1985—and there are more, too!), I went through high school relying on literacy as a tool. It served my purpose in securing grades that satisfied my parents, but was rarely something in which I would engage by choice.

The intensity of adolescence resulted in my bicycle being put away, by choice, and the search for other ways to play. Generally, there was a void. I don't think my void was particularly unique. I did everything a good adolescent probably should do. I rejected my parents; I had friends they didn't care for; I probably risked my life doing things I pray my own children do not do. And I had a senior high school English teacher, Mark Letterway, who played Simon and Garfunkel music and read us stories and invited us to read and write and think.

I would think.

I would write a little.

I didn't read much. But I did read some.

Mark Letterway was a powerful man. He was small and skinny and sometimes he got so excited that little flecks of spit shot out of his mouth when he read poetry. And he could get a class quiet when he read with an intensity that saturated the room. But I couldn't do it. I could not bring the intensity of my play life into the classroom. What would be the connection between the way I played and the activity in this classroom? It was too much of a risk. Others did, though. They would talk and explore ideas and I left that classroom with a powerful headache some days.

One assignment in that class was to write a poem. And it didn't have to rhyme. So I did. And I have no idea what it said or where it is, but I know that it was well-received. I took a private chance, on paper, and he read it and respected it. It was as though I had brought the pieces of a television set, a sprinkler, and a lawnmower to school, and he said it was good. He wrote things next to each section of the poem. He wrote the words 'powerful image.' I can't remember the image. I can remember his words. He inspired me to take a chance by playing in school and using language as the vehicle. He was the first teacher who touched me this way. I began writing poetry for play. I played hard; I wrote for hours. I wrote 10 poems in a day, about love and lust and the pain and joy and confusion of adolescence. For *play*, this was intense. And play is intense—hard, emotional, physical, spiritual, intellectual, and much more involving than most school work for me. Play is where I stretched.

The union between school and home was brief but powerful. We moved on in school to short stories and novels, but I stayed with poetry at home. It was my way. It made sense to me because it was economical. Just as I rarely brought the entire television set home because I only needed the dials, a tube, and the antenna, poetry let me use only the words I needed. I still write poetry. I still hide it from everyone because I'm afraid it does not contain powerful images. It's a vulnerable place.

Was Mark Letterway a great teacher? Does he tell stories of me, a quiet kid who, as a passive–aggressive, minimally completed assignments … except for that poetry assignment? Does he even remember me? The important part of this, for me, is just that: *me*. I remember Mark Letterway. My very personal recollection of his class is part of me when I teach, think, read, and write. A new interest in reading and writing began in that class and now permeates my life. My understanding of the nature of risk and the very personal nature of teaching and learning emanates from my construction of that memory. My growing understanding of that construction influences my teaching and learning. For that reason, I began the study of stories with my own story, a literacy autobiography.

As you read this book, I hope that you are flooded with the salient stories of *your* life, the ones you can retell and rely on as windows into your teaching, learning, and writing. The stories of our lives as teachers do not typically stand alone; they are part of the vast universe of teachers' stories. One important part of our stories is that they are about relationships that develop in our classrooms, as Don Graves (1990) explained:

> Now that I've been able to rediscover literacy for myself, I want to keep alive this new relationship with the universe. I do so by continuing to write, read, and listen to myself. Most of the time, this means sharing with others and listening to friends who explore the world in their own ways. Our dialogue helps me to be more aware of my opinions and the evidence that backs up my thinking. Obviously, we need to allow children the same opportunities we've discovered for ourselves … [because] the quality of their literacy parallels ours. (pp. 128–129)

I allow my story to grow—indeed cultivate it—throughout this book. I hope you write some of your stories along with me. You might write short stories, like those presented at the end of this chapter and in chapter 2, or you might write longer stories, like the ones in later chapters. The stories we write are the heart of who we are as teachers and learners. They are important stories and it's time to tell them.

Kathy Carter, vice president of the Division of Teaching and Teacher Education, addressed the importance of our stories at an annual convention of the American Educational Research Association. She pointed out that researchers

> have been telling stories about teaching and teacher education rather than simply reporting correlation coefficients [statistics] or generating lists of findings. This trend has been upsetting to some who mourn the loss of quantitative precision and, they would argue, scientific rigor. For many of us, however, these stories capture, more than scores or mathematical formulae ever can, the richness and indeterminacy of our experiences as teachers and the complexity of our understanding of what teaching is and how others can be prepared to engage in this profession. (Carter, 1993, p. 5)

In chapter 2, I discuss short stories, like those that teachers have typically collected over the course of their teaching and learning lives. Our short stories are rich, collected works that we accumulate, and are the ones that have taught us important lessons. Before turning to that chapter, though, the final sections of this chapter are literacy autobiographies written by teachers. I include them with the hope that you will be inspired to begin to chronicle the stories of your life—beginning with that earliest recollection—and then, perhaps, the stories of the lives in your classrooms.

The first two stories were written by undergraduate preservice teachers as part of the course requirements in the literacy block I teach. We discuss the types of evidence a literacy researcher might collect to write his or her literacy autobiography, and I explain that we meet in small groups and read our stories. Most of the students have not read their own writing aloud in many years (if ever). The day we share our literacy autobiographies is both exciting and emotionally draining for all of us. Students bring in boxes of artifacts from their literacy pasts, including books, stories, tapes of themselves reading as a child, favorite songs, interviews with parents and teachers, worksheets, workbooks, and many adventures in learning now committed to written form. There is laughter, crying, recognition of commonalities, resentment toward parents who did not save precious artifacts of their child's past, celebrations of parents who did save things, and the full range of emotions from fear to joy to sorrow to anxiety to empathy. Sharing our stories is a bonding experience; it also sets the stage for a semester of literacy study that emanates from the self toward the yet-to-be-seen classroom where students hope to teach. Our autobiographies raise questions that frame the course.

MELISSA

The first story is Melissa's.

* * *

I do not remember much about my literacy before the second grade. I found out that my mom did not either, when I was interviewing her. Mom said that she remembers reading the

Golden Books to me, especially before I began school. I guess my second-grade year sticks out in both of our minds, because that is when all my problems began.

My second-grade teacher was an old woman, probably past her retirement. I remember now, that she did not have much control over our class. Second grade is when we started really reading, or at least everyone else did. She had the class divided up into three different reading groups: low, average, and high. I, of course was in the lower group, and everyone knew what group was what. I remember coming up to the reading table (you know, the one that is shaped like a half moon?), and having everyone read a paragraph from our reading books, out loud. I hated reading, and I especially hated reading out loud! I always took the longest to read, and always had the most problems. I remember feeling sick to my stomach, and having the fear that everyone would laugh at me when it was my turn. I also remember thinking that the entire room would get quiet, when it was my turn to read, because everyone wanted to hear me make a fool out of myself.

This went on day after day, until I could not take it any more. I remember feeling really sick to my stomach every day at reading time, so one day I asked to go to the nurse's office. I convinced myself and the nurse that I was sick and I got to go home. From that day on, I spent more reading classes in the nurse's office than I did in reading. I honestly think that I was sick, but that I had mentally caused it. My teacher never offered to help me, individually, and she never figured out why I was going to the nurse's office so much. She never once informed my parents of me having problems in reading. My mom got concerned about me going to the nurse's office so much and asked my teacher at conferences if there was a problem. The teacher said no, that I was a perfect student. My parents just thought that something was happening on the bus, or that I was just having some problems with other kids.

Mom knew that reading was not coming very easy to me, but she had no idea how serious it was. I feel that 15 years ago things were a lot different between parents and the school. I do not think that they were as informed or as involved with their children's education as they might be today. My parents also worked in a larger city, but I went to a small-town school and there just was not enough time in a day to get to my school to find out what was going on.

I also feel that the fact that I am the middle child has something to do with my literacy history. I have a brother 2 years older than I and another brother 9 years younger. My younger brother has been exposed to books a lot more than my older brother and I. Ever since the day Broc was born, my mom has read to him and sung to him. She also made ABC flashcards for him, before he had even begun school. I think that my parents have been more involved in his education and made a point to talk with his teachers more than just at conferences. My parents learned a valuable lesson from me, and I am just thankful that my brother did not have to go through what I did.

I feel that I just slipped through the cracks during my entire year in second grade. Every time after second grade that I was expected to read out loud, that sick feeling came back and the fear that everyone would laugh at me did, too. What happened to me in the second grade has haunted me for the past 14 years. Reading is something that teachers are responsible for teaching children; it is something that will shape the rest of their lives. It should not be taken lightly, or overlooked at any grade. Teachers have a big responsibility to teach children something that they will use every day of their lives, and if a teacher does not face that responsibility he or she could have a negative impact on students' lives.

The following year, in third grade, my mom had a meeting with my teacher, and was surprised to hear that I was 2 years below grade level in reading. I was put into a special reading class immediately and by the end of the year I was at grade level. I am thankful that my third-grade teacher had noticed my problems right away, so that I did not have to spend another year in the nurse's office.

The only good thing that came out of this experience is that it is the driving force for me wanting to become a teacher. It was not until this year that I had come to realize this though. I have always loved children, and being with them, and I NEVER want a child to go through what I went through. My values and beliefs as a teacher are all based on my education, basically my second-grade year.

UNDERSTANDING MELISSA

Melissa's literacy autobiography became a sort of quest for her during the professional semester she spent in my class. She had not thought much about her literacy past, but in the same sentence she explains that it is her reason for becoming a teacher. Her understanding of the history that drives her—that motivates her to teach—stretched beyond her own recollection. She interviewed her parents about the situation between the home and the school and learned how intimidated her parents were of the school and, subsequently, how they overcame that intimidation to ensure her brother's success. She sought evidence for some of the intimations she felt regarding her school life. She found that her second-grade teacher retired and could not be found. She located samples of her work from her elementary school years and these helped to bring back memories. Melissa was making sense of her literacy life so that she could make sense of her teaching life.

As we tell our stories, we start with what is important to us. We start with what we remember most because of the energy and baggage attached to those recollections. Melissa explored her literacy life in the present, too. She talked with me about a change she was feeling as she spent time writing in her required journal and reading professional books. She learned that she needed to organize her time to have large blocks available for reading and writing. Rather than condemn her reading process, she began to systematically explore it to see when she felt best about reading. Although the discoveries she made will probably not rock the world of reading researchers, they have subtly changed her outlook. She has become open to studying her students' literacy lives when she is a teacher and to sharing her own literacy life with them. She has come to view a literacy life as pliable, but not something that will change dramatically at once. It is something that can change, and that change is something she experienced herself.

It helped Melissa to read Shelley Harwayne's (1992) book in which children's literacy lives are viewed as integral parts of classroom literacy life:

> Wouldn't I be a better teacher knowing that Stacey has a storytelling family? ... Wouldn't I be a better teacher of reading and writing because I appreciated the fact that literate acts are different in different families? ...
>
> The more we know about our students, the easier it becomes to teach wisely and well. We need to begin the school year by bringing children's lives—their family photos

and family stories, their hobbies and their collections—into the classroom. We also need to start the year by getting to know our students' life lines as readers and writers. …

Our students bring more than backpacks and lunch boxes to school. (p. 30)

Melissa's study of herself initiated her into the very personal nature of the growth inherent in storytelling and encouraged her to take the risk and begin reading and writing in an authentic way.

LYDIA

Lydia is quite different from Melissa. Lydia looks at the writing of her literacy autobiography as a challenging way to uncover and make sense of her past. As part of locating evidence of her journey into her literacy life, Lydia found a photo of herself writing, two stories she wrote in school, an illustrated story she did at home, a diary she kept in school, old report cards, a story that she wrote for the Young Author's Contest, and a children's book she wrote in eighth grade. She pointed out that there was much evidence of her literacy development saved by her parents and that she selected items that showed growth or stirred memories.

* * *

I have never been asked to think about my past literacy and language development. Yes, there are many times when I am required to try to remember back to my distant past and recall an event, but usually it does not correlate with how I have been shaped to become the person I am. Therefore, as I was presented with the idea of writing a literacy autobiography I was quite excited about having the opportunity to look into my past and try to pull things out that have made me become the literate person I am. Today, as a young adult, I enjoy both reading and writing to the point that these are the type of activities I would choose to do in my spare time. Yet I never thought about why I enjoy reading and writing until I began to search through my past and see patterns that developed when I was young.

My mother is an avid reader. She reads anything and everything that she can get her hands on. She could read an entire book in a few hours and completely comprehend the entire book. Consequently, her knowledge is incredible. Over dinner, she will throw out facts and information that come from her great "wisdom base," and totally shock the family as we recognize our own stupidity. Her love for books and knowledge was evident to me when I was a young child. As I talked to my parents about their role in my literacy development, I discovered some interesting things. From birth, my mom read books to me. I do remember when I was 7 or 8 that every night before bed my mom would read my sister and me a chapter out of a book. The books that were read to me at this time that I recall most vividly were the *Chronicles of Narnia* by C. S. Lewis (these books still hold a place in my heart). To me, these were very special memories because it really made my relationship with my mother special and unique. My mother also told me that she consistently read to me when I was a baby, toddler, and preschooler. What great exposure to reading and language I had before I entered school! My father also read to me occasionally. Since he and my mom have been married, he has learned to enjoy reading. Thus, today he reads quite consistently to increase his knowledge and as a way to grasp my mom's passion in life.

My parents told me that I really enjoyed books and reading when I was young. Actually, I can remember my first favorite book as a child. It was called *Now I Am Two*. It was about a little girl named Judy who just turned 2 and all the things she could do as a 2-year-old. I am sure I was around this age when it was first read to me and it continued to be my favorite book for years because I could relate to it. I also remember I liked a book called *Where Did The Little Girl Go?* This book was about a baby who had grown up and had seen her baby picture. She then searched all around the house looking for the little baby until finally her mother told her that she was the little baby in the picture. I liked this book because I was at the age where I could understand that once I was a baby and that I was growing up. I think this book helped me deal with grasping the concept of getting older and changing with age. I think these books began my pattern for an interest in books that teach me about something relevant to my circumstance. Even today I look for books that will help me in certain areas of my life or that will help me grow to become a better person.

My parents were not really sure how I started to read, and I really cannot remember ever learning how to read. My mom told me that I most likely learned to read when I was in preschool. I was turning 5 when I entered preschool because my birthday was in early November and I had missed the public school deadline for entry into kindergarten. Apparently, I knew my alphabet when I went to preschool and my mother thinks that my preschool teacher began teaching basic sounds of letters as well as putting letters together to make words. Therefore, when I entered kindergarten I think I was already able to comprehend and read some words. (My younger and only sister had an incredibly difficult time reading. She struggled with spelling and reading all throughout grade school and I wonder if it had to do with her age of entry.) Perhaps one thing that heavily influences children's abilities to learn to read and write is their age and state of maturity. When I was 5, I was definitely ready for kindergarten, but when my sister was 5 she was not yet ready to dive into the scheme of reading and writing.

In school I do not think that I ever learned phonics. If I did learn phonics, I certainly do not remember any of the rules involved. I guess I was taught to sound out some words as well as learn to recognize other words. I think it is highly probable that I learned to read whole words because of my visualization abilities. All throughout school I have had an incredible ability to be able to memorize how things look visually. Many times, after I read something, I am able to memorize how things look visually and I can recall some of that information by visualizing where the information was on the page. Perhaps this accounts for the fact that I have never had any difficulty with spelling because I am usually able to visualize the word after the first time I see it.

After talking to my parents and pressing my brain to try to remember everything I could, I decided to venture into "The Box." This box was started by my parents when I was young as a means to keep a lot of the things I did in my life in elementary school (there is some junior high and high school stuff in it also). To me this was the real exciting part of my journey to trace my literacy roots. There were some things that I remembered doing and other things that I do not remember at all. During my search I discovered my development from some of my teachers' points of view.

I was able to dig up a lot of old report cards from my elementary teachers and they contained information about my reading and language arts development. In 1979 (I was 7 years old), my teacher said that I was progressing well in letter recognition as well as expressing myself with confidence in the classroom. My goals for 1979 were to write my letters and tell time. In 1980, the teacher said that I was excited about reading and that I was forming good comprehension skills. In the language arts area I was becoming aware of how to form good sentences. It is recorded that some of my skill levels and progress fluctuated throughout the years (which I do not think is a very good indication of learning). The one thing that stayed consistent, however, was my spelling. I was always able to spell well and my teachers indicated that I had little trouble in formulating words.

Along with these reports by teachers, I still have many of the stories I have written and the things I did relating to literacy. How much fun it is to look back on these treasures! I have spent a lot of time laughing in the last few days as I have sorted through some things. I am definitely grateful that my parents kept these things for me to look back on. There were a few observations I made from digging through my past. First of all, it seemed that I frequently wrote about tragedy and problems. Perhaps I was taught that there needs to be some sort of problem to be solved in a story. Even today I find the most fascinating books and movies the ones that involve deep plots and tragedy. I think this is an important part of my literacy because I can now see that the way that I read and write today is really directly related to how I read and wrote as a youngster. Of course my world of literacy has expanded and continues to expand over time but it is interesting to see where I have come from.

I also noticed in my stories and papers that there were times when the teacher corrected my mistakes with THE "red ink or blue ink." How humiliating it is to see all my mistakes and errors marked for the world to see. I also noted that in most of my pieces what was emphasized was grammatical structure rather than content or individual growth. When I was in second or third grade (I think) I wrote a story called, "Cindy's Problem." I entered this story in a contest and earned second place. As I read this story, I realized that there were many structural errors and grammatical mistakes. Yet none of them were scribbled out by a red pen and I was able to turn in my piece as is. I remember being so excited and proud of my story because I felt that I had done a good job. Certainly it did no harm for my teacher not to correct my work and, in fact, I think it was a boost of confidence for me as I saw that I could accomplish something and achieve my goals.

Today as a reader and writer I have done so much more than I ever would have expected. First of all, I love to write. It is the type of thing that is almost addictive. When I am journaling or writing letters, I get so into it that I really do not want to put it down. I think writing is such a release for me and helps me to sort through my feelings and draw conclusions about my own life. I have noticed though that sometimes when I write my mind works so fast that I tend to run words together or leave letters off words because thoughts come to my mind so quickly. This year I have also ventured into the world of writing poetry because I took a university course. This was a new and unique way of expression that I had not seriously indulged in before last semester. Poetry gave me new insight into the world and how I see and perceive things around me. Secondly, I love to read. In my spare time (that is if I ever have any) I enjoy reading. Some of the time I read fiction—strictly for pleasure—or other times I read books that deal with issues that I am interested in knowing more about. I read fairly fast and have noticed that sometimes I lack gaining total comprehension of what I read.

I guess now that I have somewhat traced the roots of my literacy it is time for me to start to think about how I can continue to grow in my literacy so that I can better help my future students. It is really hard for me to think about the fact that I will help shape the patterns of learning and growth for other students. I am wondering what ways are best for learning. I tend to agree with Graves that learning about literary has to be seen and practiced rather than graded and corrected. I think it is important that students feel confident about their abilities and that they are able to set goals they will be able to reach.

I certainly have progressed since my elementary years. Learning to read and write was something that opened up my world and continues to open up new and exciting opportunities. I anticipate beginning with where my literacy level is now and embarking on ways in which I can grow into someone who is constantly aware of my literacy knowledge and capabilities. After all, how can I expect my students to learn anything if I am not willing to learn with them?

UNDERSTANDING LYDIA

I asked Lydia what she learned from writing her literacy autobiography. She sent me a written response:

> I certainly learned a lot. I developed conclusions on patterns of reading/writing that have been continuous since my younger years!! I see the impact of learning to read and write on how one reads and writes as a youngster. And I now can see how my literacy roots will affect my teaching. Because I now know a little more about myself, I can help my students learn to discover things about themselves as well as help them learn about literacy.

As a successful reader and writer, Lydia ventures into looking for patterns across time. She is different from Melissa, but they are both beginning to collect their literate lives. As they begin to teach, they will collect their experiences with children in their classrooms and schools. Their collections are an important part of the foundation they will use to make sense of their teaching and learning lives. Lydia's story of her development as a reader and writer also provided many questions about 'good' readers and 'good' writers; her questions helped frame the issues we addressed in the course.

TRACI: MY NOSE IS STUCK IN A BOOK AND OTHER LITERACY STORIES

Traci teaches middle school and was a graduate student in a summer session course I taught. I had read *Interwoven Conversations* by Judith Newman (1991), in which she worked with teachers to describe and make sense of their literacy lives as one way to understand classroom life. The teachers in her class become quite committed to writing their lives, as well as the lives of their students. The teachers see that understanding themselves and their students are two important facets of teaching and learning. One teacher wrote:

> I have come to believe there are two reasons for engaging in reflection: to get to know my students better, to understand what they are doing and experiencing; and to learn more about myself as a researcher. (p. 355)

I called the summer course "Collective Literacies: The Reading/Writing Lives of Children and Teachers" and it was modeled after Newman's book. Very quickly, though, the course took on its own life (and I was glad it did). Some of the class members decided to write literacy autobiographies, whereas others explored different issues of literacy relevant to their classrooms. In this section, Traci's literacy autobiography is presented. Cindy, another member of the class, wrote a literacy autobiography that is presented as the final piece in this chapter.

* * *

I've always had my nose stuck in a book. I've always loved to read and it seems there has never been enough time for me to read all the books I've wanted to. I could read forever. But my own literacy journey began long before I could decipher the printed word.

My parents divorced when I was in fourth grade, and from that point on I lived with my mom. My memories of my dad and I before this time stick out in my head like a perfectly clear vision. We had our stories, my dad and I. He used to tell me this story about this squirrel looking for its nuts that it had hidden and couldn't remember where. His two fingers were the squirrel and it would look for the nuts behind my ears, in my hair, in my armpits. It would always find those nuts in my bellybutton. The point of the whole thing was to tickle me until I shrieked with laughter but it's not so much the tickling I remember. It is the story.

Also, when I was little, I had these pink pajamas with the number 5 on the front. My dad had this poem about those pajamas that he said to me every single night. It was a strange nonsense poem but I loved it because it was mine. It went something like this:

Good old number 5,
Hardly a many now alive
That doesn't remember
Good ole' number 5.
He fought the fit and fit the fought
with his good ole' forks, knives, and spoons.

It wasn't until years later that I came across a Civil War poem that was very similar to my poem about good ole' number 5. My dad had taken that poem and made it funny for me.

After my parents' divorce, my brother and sister went to live with my dad and I moved with my mom. In a way, I became an only child and spent most of my waking hours reading. As a child, I had loved the library and as an adolescent, it remained my favorite place.

I loved series books and read all the *Trixie Belden*, all the *Nancy Drew*, and all of the *Little House on the Prairie* books. It felt like a great accomplishment that I had read every single book. Books were like an escape for me. I didn't have to deal with my parents' divorce, my mom's new boyfriend, or what the town was saying about the whole thing. Books took me anywhere I wanted to go and I didn't have to justify that to anyone.

I read anywhere and everywhere, almost to the point of being antisocial. We would go to a family reunion and my relatives would remark that I always had my nose stuck in a book. I told my mom the books were always more interesting than my Kansas relatives.

My reading habits developed early, although I'm still not sure how they became such strong habits. My parents do not read. In fact, I can't ever recall seeing my mom read a book. And it seems amazing that my own literacy habits have grown out of a need to entertain myself as a youngster. Although, if this is truly how I developed literacy, it gives me hope for all my students whose only exposure to books and libraries is at school.

My writing history began, again, about the time of my parents' divorce. I started keeping a diary but it was a pretty mundane step-by-step account of each day's happenings. Then, when I moved, my only contact with my friends was through letters. I began to write creative, silly, out-of-this-world letters because I thought my friends back home would stop writing if they did not really like the letters I was sending. My first exposure to audience!

I knew exactly who my audience was and I milked them for all they were worth. Needless to say, all but a few of them stopped writing after a couple of months.

I can remember three teachers in high school who impacted my literacy life. The first was my sophomore English teacher. His initials were E. Z., but he was far from easy, maybe one of the hardest teachers I've ever had. But he pushed me to my limits and he encouraged me to do my best. He gave me confidence that I was a good writer; it's funny that we can't get that confidence from ourselves. I left his class believing I could write.

Killer Keller (that is what we called her and her red pen) convinced me I couldn't write. This was an advanced composition class. We read *Walden* and instead of discussing its social implications or what it meant for us, she asked us questions on the text like, "How many bushels of corn did Thoreau take to town?" Pretty meaningless, rote memory types of things. I would get my red ink-stained essays back from her and never even look at them. Why should I? There was no opportunity to correct my mistakes.

Lucky for me, I was also in a creative writing class. Mr. E was on the cutting edge of writing workshop. He let us write whatever we wanted. He encouraged us and made our writing lives important. It's scary how teachers can influence lives, for better or worse.

It seems I could document thousands of incidents in my life that helped me develop into a reader and writer. I have always had a wild imagination, beginning with the make-believe friend I had when I was little. Her name was Sarafina and I was always reading to her and telling her stories. I believe that the way I think and perceive things has a lot do to with my literacy history. The things I have learned though reading and writing influence the way I live and think. It is this message that I try to give my students: that these reading and writing events can really be life-changing. More than certain events, I think reading and writing are just a way of life for me. I hope everyone will continue to say that I always have my nose stuck in a book. My husband said it just last night.

UNDERSTANDING TRACI

Traci's past (literacy and otherwise) is remarkable. She shows how her father cultivated her sense of story with love, affection, touch, humor, and joy. She remembers her parents not reading, but she found reading as a way of continuing the pleasure she found in stories. Relate Traci's literacy autobiography to yourself, to your life. Perhaps you find some similarities that will inspire you to write. Do you remember which stories or songs or poems were "yours"—special for you and someone else? Or, perhaps your life is so different from Traci's that you are motivated to write because of the contrast between her life and yours. Or, maybe reading others' stories and analyzing them is the way you begin to write your own stories. All of these are good reasons to write and ways to become a writer.

ANNA: GROWING OUT OF THE CRIB

Cindy decided to present her literacy life by focusing on one important facet of it, the move out of her crib. Perhaps her writing will inspire you to create your literacy autobiography as a poem, story, song, dance, work of art, sculpture, or in other important medium. Notice that Cindy uses a different name (Anna) as she presents a part of her life to us; that's a writer's license that you can use, too.

Growing
out of the
Crib

Written
and
illustrated
by
Cindy Brown

Growing out of the Crib

Written
and
illustrated
by
Cindy Brown

1994

For all of us with stories to tell.

She heard her mother descending the staircase. When the third to the last stair creaked, Anna knew that for the fifth night in a row, she had tricked her parents. When Anna was supposed to be drifting off to sleep while her mother read, she only closed her eyes.

She wanted to make her sleeping
believable, so she added heavy breathing and
an occasional twitch. (This she picked up
from watching their beagle).

The hardest part of her trick came when her mother carried her from the rocking chair to her crib across the room. Anna, who had always been the most tickle-sensitive three year old in the neighborhood, really had to force herself not to giggle.

It was after she heard the light switch
and felt the room darken that she realized
she had succeeded. Anna waited until she
heard the sewing machine to make her move.
(She knew when the sewing machine's hum
controlled by her mother joined the tapping
type writer controlled by her father, they
would be kept busy downstairs).

Cuddling her trusty stuffed sidekick, Lambie, Anna started climbing out of her crib. Guided by the rectangle of light that flowed from the hallway, she carefully placed her right foot between the slats of the crib. She swung her left leg up and over the top railing. After planting her left foot between the slats on the outside, she quickly flung over her other leg.

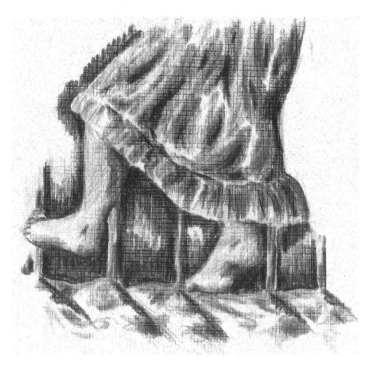

The crib rattled and swayed slightly as she reached for the cold tile with her toes. Once she lowered herself to the floor, she turned and looked towards the door. She expected to see her parents standing there, upset because of her late-night climbing. Only the light peeked in.

Anna smiled as she walked towards her destination: the bookcase. She padded lightly across the tile and squatted in front of her books, gently setting Lambie down. Tonight, she would take even more books than last night.

After stacking six books in her arms, she reached for Lambie. As she lowered her arm, two books slid from the pile in her arms and fell with thuds to the floor. Anna froze! She hoped that noise wasn't heard downstairs! She listened as the sewing machine and type writer became silent. Anna took a deep breath when she heard them start again a few seconds later because she knew this had been a close call!

Anna picked up the books that had fallen
and carefully held on to everything this time.
She slowly crept across the creaking floor to
the rectangle of light. She sat down and
sorted through the books and decided the
order in which she would read them.

Then, with Lambie seated on her lap, she
began. She would read quietly to her friend,
explaining little details he might have
missed. She pointed and whispered at the
illustrations, finding delight in her
discoveries.

Anna enjoyed her private reading time, but somewhere between stories three and six, she drifted off to sleep. She didn't remember putting the books quietly back or climbing back into the crib with Lambie. She however, woke up in her crib that morning!

Whether Anna's parents heard her sneaking out of her crib to read, she was never quite sure. The very next week, however, Anna's crib was replaced with a bed.

ANNA ... AND BEYOND

Anna's story (by Cindy) is not written exactly as it occurred, but it is her recollection of the events enhanced by who she is now—a reader, writer, teacher, and more. Rather than rely on her own life, Cindy wanted to intertwine her lived experiences with a best case scenario to show how she was supported as a reader. She didn't use her real name in the story she wrote; this gave her permission to change different parts of what she had lived and remembered to develop a story that is a metaphor for the roots of her literate life. She took her license as an author quite seriously in presenting a story that gives insights into who she is, what she believes, and how she felt supported in the early years of her literacy development.

You might feel that some of the stories in chapter 1 have gaps or holes or even wide and unexplained spaces. These are the places that you and I would begin to talk; they are the windows for conversation. I hope they inspire you to write, to share your writing, and to talk. These are the ways our stories cultivate our growth.

Are you writing yet?

chapter 2

Short Stories

Aunt Sue has a head full of stories.
Aunt Sue has a whole heart full of stories.
Summer nights on the front porch
Aunt Sue cuddles a brown-faced child to her bosom
And tells him stories.

Black slaves
Working in the hot sun,
And black slaves
Walking in the dewy night,
And black slaves
Singing sorrow songs on the banks of a mighty river
Mingle themselves softly
In the flow of old Aunt Sue's voice,
Mingle themselves softly
In the dark shadows that cross and recross
Aunt Sue's stories.

And the dark-faced child, listening,
Knows that Aunt Sue's stories are real stories.
He knows that Aunt Sue never got her stories
Out of any book at all,
But that they came
Right out of her own life.

The dark-faced child is quiet
Of a summer night
Listening to Aunt Sue's stories.

—Hughes (1967)

Teachers have heads full of stories that come right out of our own lives. We listen to each others' stories in amazement and wonder. David Wilson, a colleague of mine at the University of Nebraska, Lincoln, said that one teacher will often answer a colleague's story with another story. One of the powerful facets of Langston Hughes' poem is that it is reminiscent of teachers' stories because it is economical. By "economical," I mean that the poem uses few words, but evokes images that are large, colorful, and even have a sense of heat and humidity. A few words go a long way. Teachers' stories are often required to be economical. We just do not have the time to cultivate a story, to frame it, and to tell it with all its subtleties and related pieces. We abbreviate the story to 'get it out,' sometimes in an almost crisis-like, therapeutic fashion. Our telling of brief, quick, or short stories about our teaching lives grounds us after an intense day. This is an economical use of stories as a vent for the joys and sorrows and as a way to come to terms with our days.

We need to honor our short stories because of their economical nature and because, when cultivating a discussion, we often find that the stories run deep—from the head and from the heart.

Two important things I learned since becoming a teacher educator and researcher are that stories are more complex than I expected (especially when we frame them in some way); and many teachers already know about this and have been framing their stories for years. By "framing," I mean reading and thinking about others' writings and making sense of my stories through the lenses of that reading and thinking. I did that to some degree in chapter 1, when I incorporated Kohl's thinking into my own story. His story and mine resonated to such a degree that I wanted to weave his into mine. It's okay to do this. I used to feel disappointed when I read someone who wrote ideas that I loved. "Why didn't I write that first?" I would ask myself. Now, as I read, I find myself thinking, "That fits with my thinking and way of being. It serves as a frame for my own story." This way of thinking is more comfortable and seems to empower me as I find support for my *Self* in others' work.

One of the joys of teaching graduate and undergraduate language and literacy courses has been the use of my stories—recollections from more than 15 years of teaching in the elementary school. Certain children and events are quite salient because they taught me so much. The time I spent reflecting on my teaching practices (Dewey, 1939; Schon, 1987) led me to understand my stories (my experiences) in terms of various theories. Stories make theory real.

Vivian Paley's (1981) stories of a boy named Wally are one example of that. Vivian told many short stories of Wally as he lived and learned in her classroom and school. Her understanding of Wally's actions become clear in and through the stories she told. Each story is an important vehicle by which she makes sense of her own teaching and learning as well as serving as documentation of Wally's growth. These short stories teach the teacher.

This chapter is a blend of some of the theory that I am reading, discovering, uncovering, recovering, and confirming, and the language stories (Harste,

Woodward, & Burke, 1984) that have stayed with me over the years of my experiences in schools and the communities in which they are situated. I have tried to weave together two facets to this chapter. First, there are the stories from my classroom life with children and beyond. Second, I frame the stories within the work of other teachers and researchers. As we collect and analyze our stories and share them, we gain insights into the language and literacy processes that saturate our classrooms.

LEO

The following paragraph is a brief frame of the story of Leo. A frame may be brief or extensive. A brief frame tells readers that I am reading others' work to make sense of my own. It informs you of the perspective I am taking on the story that is being presented by mentioning the names of people whose work I've read, and offers a glimpse of my understanding of that work and how it fits, supports, extends, or elaborates the story I am telling. A more extensive frame would involve a much more in-depth search of the literature. As the researcher and storyteller, I can search as much as I like, usually to the point of satisfying myself and my perceived interests of my audience. Each of the stories that follow is put into a perspective (*contextualized*) by the brief frames in the introductory paragraphs. Sometimes we weave the frames throughout our stories, other times we may decide to put them all in one place. These are decisions you make as the storyteller, trying to keep your audience in mind as you do so.

The teachers and researchers cited here are the ones who help me understand what happened in my very first classroom. Children are constantly making meaning (Wells, 1986) in ways that fascinate the active kidwatcher (Goodman, 1985). Their cultures and lives permeate our classrooms and, as we continually sensitize ourselves to the diversity of individuals who enter our rooms, we find ways in which they can meet safely and remain well-rooted in who they are. The language children learn in school is unique (Cazden, 1988; Mehan, 1982) and does not always reflect language as it is used out of school. With that as a brief frame, let's look at Leo.

Leo was one of the last students I noticed when I began my student teaching assignment at a Head Start program in New York City. He was quiet and, I later learned, secure in who he was. As my student teaching progressed, I learned more and more about each of the children's likes and dislikes. Our large room was organized into centers: blocks, play kitchen, water and sand, and more. The play kitchen had a box full of old clothing and a wonderful assortment of hats. The children's interest in the centers changed over the course of the semester. One child or group might get involved in the block center and play for 4 or 5 consecutive days at that center. Interest might change to the kitchen area and various roles would emerge and shift as different scenarios unfolded.

Leo's role in each of the centers rarely involved speaking. He listened and seemed to talk with his eyes and hands. A strong look from Leo was interpreted as his desire to have a leading role in what was unfolding. His presence meant he was participating in whatever capacity he wanted to. Leo often pointed or just took what he wanted when he was playing. The children accepted this and rarely took any action to prevent Leo from doing what he chose. He was a little smaller than the other 4-year-olds in our room, but he had a quiet sense of presence, respected by all the children in some unspoken way that I did not understand.

The children in this room loved stories, and my cooperating teacher and I loved to read them. We read many stories, old and new, and often read them many times in a given day or week. Occasionally, interest in a story led to a dramatic interpretation of it. So it was with *Caps for Sale* (Slobodkina, 1943).

I read the story to the children and they laughed and laughed as I stood up and read the part of the frustrated peddler. I wagged my finger in the air and jumped up and down and pointed to the imaginary monkeys, "You monkeys, you. Give me back my caps!" Then I switched roles and became the monkeys imitating the frustrated peddler. So it went, back and forth, until the peddler finally throws his own hat to the ground and the monkeys follow suit. The laughter in the room was rich and warmed me in deep places. So, when the call came to read it again, I certainly did.

One of the children suggested we act out the story. This was not unusual, and we discussed what we needed and who would take which parts. One child went to the dress up box and brought out all the hats. We had a movable staircase with three steps. That would serve as the tree. We retold the story and most of the children decided they wanted to be monkeys. Leo stood up, put his hands on his waist, and said, "I'll be the peddler." I was so pleased that he verbally volunteered to be involved. There was a nod of heads as the other children in the class agreed to have Leo be the peddler.

Everything was set. Leo had all the hats piled high on his head. The staircase "tree" was in place and all the monkeys were silently waiting in it. "Caps for sale!" Leo screamed as he walked around the room. He walked to the kitchen center and the block center and all the other empty areas of the room looking for individuals to buy his caps. As he left each center, he would shake his head from side to side in disgust at not having sold a single cap. Finally, he arrived at the tree. He looked around and stretched and looked in all directions again. Seeing no one, he sat down, leaning on the side of the stairs, and went to sleep.

As Leo the cap peddler slept, all of the monkeys quietly came down from the tree. They each approached Leo, looked hard at his face to make sure that he was sleeping, and then carefully removed one of his caps and placed it on their own head. They looked at each other with the caps on their heads and quietly went back up the tree. Leo slept. And slept. I began to wonder if he had indeed really fallen asleep. The children were more patient that I was and seemed to trust how long Leo chose to be 'asleep.' Soon, he stirred and moved his head from side to side. Then he opened his eyes and rubbed them, as though he had truly been asleep. I had no idea he was such an actor.

Leo rose and stretched. He stretched again and scratched his belly through his shirt. He smacked his lips as though they were dry from a long and deep nap. Then, Leo put his hands to his head to make sure that the pile of caps was still there. He seemed genuinely surprised that the caps were gone. Leo looked to the left and to the right and all around the room, except for up in the tree. He scratched his head and put his hand to his chin as though trying to remember where he might have placed that pile of caps.

Leo finally looked at the tree. He lifted his head and eyes slowly to the top and he looked at the monkeys up in the tree. They had loved his performance up until that point. They had giggled as he looked in each of the centers and particularly delighted in his scratching his belly. Now, their eyes met. We all anticipated what would happen next, as we had each time I reread the story.

Leo looked at the monkeys hard. Then he felt the top of his head one more time. He looked back at the monkeys, pointed his finger at the group and said, "You motherfucking monkeys. You give me back my goddamn hats." The monkeys paused for a moment—as did the student teacher—and then they threw their hats down.

"Oh, let's do it again," Lisa said with a rich and satisfied voice.

"I, uhhh, mmm," I said.

"I'll be the peddler," Stanley half said and asked looking at Leo.

Leo nodded yes.

The hats were gathered for Stanley and the children started the story reenactment for the second time. Subsequent reenactments followed the book more closely in language and sequence and received equal satisfaction from the actors. It occurred to me that I was the only one who was genuinely surprised at what had happened. I thought about that a lot on the way home.

As a student teacher, I was constantly making choices about what was happening in the classroom. My cooperating teacher gave me many opportunities to enact my decisions, a responsibility I did not take lightly. I could not always articulate why I did something; now, as a teacher educator, I find myself constantly dealing with helping others make sense of their decisions. Stories such as this one about Leo are often the vehicle for the initiation of a process of articulation.

Leo was using the language of his home and community, the community of his classmates, and the broader community in which he lived. He spoke with none of the awareness of the registers (Halliday, 1978) I either intuited or was taught as a student from a middle-class home. A *register* is a way of speaking that is specific to an individual within a context (I'll discuss this more in a bit). I knew that language in school and language at home were different; Leo was not demonstrating such an awareness.

The children were not surprised at his use of specific words and his lack of adherence to the story as it was told in the book because they knew Leo in ways that they could not express. They knew he was also quite present, and when he spoke, they paid close attention to what he said. They seemed to know the words he spoke, had heard them before, and didn't think they were out of place, even though they might not have used those words themselves.

I made sense of Leo's use of language by reading Michael Halliday. Halliday (1978) discussed field, tenor, and mode of oral language. The field consists of the physical setting, the time, and the particular subject matter a speaker is discussing. We were in school, doing a play during the school day. The tenor is the nature of the relationships between those present. The mode, in this case, was oral language. Field, tenor, and mode define the register a speaker uses. For example, when I teach a university course, my physical movements, the fact that we are in a university classroom, the nature of the relationships I have with the students, and the subject matter we are addressing all contribute to the register of the speech acts. I usually try to be somewhat informal, but there are certain ways of speaking that I would not use. Yet, when friends arrive at my home, I might use a distinctively different register.

Leo's choice of words demonstrated that he did not know certain rules of discourse for school. Or, perhaps he did know the rules, but chose to ignore them. Either way, as the student teacher working with the cooperating teacher, I had to make certain decisions about language. I decided that I would try to learn more about oral language as it was used in the classroom. Most immediately, I found myself becoming reflective about issues of oral language, particularly words that trigger responses within me. This is something I encourage my undergraduates to do as they pursue field experiences in a variety of classrooms. The ways in which children use language ultimately becomes a topic of discussion because of grammar, 'bad words,' spelling, or other language issues.

I hope that the stories in this chapter stimulate discussion about the issues inherent in each story and encourage preservice and inservice teachers to begin collecting and writing stories from their own experiences to analyze. My own adventures with language were just beginning.

HOW LOW CAN YOU GO?

The relationships among language, literacy, and culture were about to become more salient for me as I moved from New York City to rural New York. I was naive about language and its relationship to context (Halliday, 1978) when I began my first teaching job there.

The first year I taught was in a rural part of New York State. The school, a few years before, had secured a federal grant to help children having difficulty learning to read. As part of the grant, the school was allowed to build two new classrooms for the struggling readers. The area below the cafeteria was dug out and the rooms were added there. They were in the lowest part of the school, a metaphor of which I was often reminded as teachers would say, "Fred, it's time for you to go down to reading with Mr. Meyer."

The program was a pull-out program in which I saw children for 45 minutes a day. The pull-out program was clearly not the best design for the fourth through sixth graders with whom I worked, but this was my first teaching job outside of New York City and I was thrilled to have it. There were many curricular issues with which I had to deal, such as not using basal readers with kids who were so frustrated using them over the past 5 to 8 years. I had more to learn than curricula, however.

Things were moving along quite well, I thought. Children were listening to contemporary music, writing stories, designing various art projects, even building birdhouses by reading and following directions. It seemed as though we understood each other and they knew that my classroom was a safe place in which they could discuss many things. I liked to think, even prided myself in the fact, that we were explorers, learning about and sharing our worlds.

One day, near the middle of October, Fred asked, "Mr. Meyer, may I go to the basement?"

"Fred," I said, "this is the basement. The building stops here."

He looked at me as though I had lost my mind. "No," he said, "I need to use the basement."

"What would you use it for?" I asked, feeling confident that we were exploring something we could figure out together.

Fred looked at me hard. He rolled his eyes, then went back to reading the book he had chosen. A little while later, Fred was back. He looked a lot more anxious than he had looked earlier and said, "I really need the basement."

I was flattered. I thought that he needed me and viewed the room as a safe place for him to learn and grow. "Oh," I said.

"Mr. Meyer!" Fred's voice was louder than I had ever heard it before. "I really need to use the basement right now."

"Mr. Meyer, the basement is the bathroom," Lisa shouted across the room.

"What?" I asked. "The basement is the bathroom? That doesn't make any sense."

"Can I use the base ... the bathroom?" Fred asked.

"Yes, of course, go ahead," I said.

I learned that when houses in this part of New York first installed indoor plumbing, it was typically put in the basement, where pipes had less of a chance of freezing.

This is a story that might be framed for understanding by considering the idea that no text is free of a context. Halliday and Hasan (1985) referred to text and *con-text* to emphasize that text goes along with (hence the prefix) a place where that text unfolds: context. A text can never exist without a context. Words never stand alone outside of a context. We can imagine all the books in the library, for example, but they do not become text until they are in a relationship with others—a context. One word, then, such as *basement* is different across contexts.

This leads to a discussion of texts, even single words as texts, which are always embedded in a context. What significance does this have for teaching or learning? Quite a bit when we realize that we rely on words to make meaning, but the words we use have such a broad spectrum of meaning that we might not always be understood as we intend. Intention, text, and context are inextricably intertwined. As teachers, we are often busy teasing out the meaning that children make of our intentions.

JEANNIE

My story about Jeannie is framed in the belief that the use of basal reading systems does more than limit children's exposure to good literature and good teaching (Goodman, Shannon, Freeman, & Murphy, 1987). The basal, by its very nature, sets up a classroom process with specific structures of participation (Philips, 1971) that ignore, deny, or even undermine success in reading (Au, 1981). Basals can also disempower teachers and children who believe, as I did, that basals teach reading.

My second year of teaching was in a second-grade class; I had begged the principal to consider me for that job. I had dreamed of being a primary-level teacher and this was my chance. He was not thrilled with the idea and was hesitant to suggest it to the Board of Education because no male had ever taught children younger than fifth graders in this school. I encouraged him to explain to the Board that I was a reading specialist and, as such, would offer the children a strong start in reading, particularly those who were experiencing difficulty. That was a strong selling point for me and I was given the job.

Two weeks before school opened, I decided that not only did I not know anything about teaching reading, I didn't know anything about teaching anything to anyone. Panic set in. I ran to the first-grade teacher and explained my dilemma. She was instrumental in calming me down.

"First," she said, speaking from 20 years of first-grade experience, "remember that you are bigger than they are."

I thought this would be good to remember. It worked pretty well, too, as far as keeping order was concerned. Well, it worked until we read *Charlie and the Chocolate Factory* (Dahl, 1964). We got to the part where the spoiled child, Veruca Salt, broke into the nut room to take a trained squirrel for her own. The 25 squirrels in the nut room quickly formed groups, each group grabbing a different limb, with the last squirrel knocking Veruca on the head, deciding she was a bad nut, and sending her down the garbage chute. I began to wonder. Couldn't a group of children do the same thing to almost any adult? Fortunately for me, that never happened.

"Second," my colleague who taught first grade said, "to teach reading you go to the table outside of the principal's office and get your piles."

"Piles?" I asked.

"Yes, you use those piles for your reading groups."

Outside of the principal's office was a long table. I located the "Meyer" pile and took it to my classroom to make sense of it. It was actually three piles. Each pile was a stack of workbooks from the basal reader, tied together with a string. I cut the string and examined the first pile. It was a pile of first-grade reading workbooks, all completed to page 36. The second pile was a different first-grade reading workbook set, completed to page 76. The third pile was new second-grade reading workbooks. I brought the piles back to the veteran teacher.

"Yes, those are your groups. We formed them last year. The other first-grade teacher and I made sure that we stopped in the same place with our groups so that we could mix the kids up for second grade."

This made sense to me at the time. How thoughtful. They worked to stop in the same place so that I could pick up where they left off. So, reading was organized and ready to go. I had the teacher's guides in another pile and I read through those before the first day. It all seemed so simple and soothed my fears about teaching reading. The guides had three different fonts. A normal font indicated what I should say verbatim to the children; the bold font was for directions to me, such as "Pass out the children's reading books"; the italicized printing was for responses to questions that the teacher's guide told me to ask.

The children came and I was a primary-level teacher. They were super and I was thrilled and things were moving right along. The basal 'worked.' The kids seemed to be learning the prescribed vocabulary and they were mastering the skills. I had three reading groups and most days went like clockwork, as I spent 20 to 30 minutes per group.

Toward the middle of October, we were all getting very comfortable with one another. The children would sometimes hug me good-bye as they left the reading table or would lean on me when they had finished reading a section and were waiting politely. I had my top group at the reading table. Jeannie and Jeanna were best friends and both were in this group. One sat on one side of me and the other sat on the other. Jeannie was the fastest reader in the group and had great comprehension. She was also a very polite 'waiter.'

On this particular day, we were reading a story from the basal. We 'read the pictures' and I introduced new vocabulary using flashcards. Then, the children were instructed to read the first three pages, paying close attention for the answers to some questions I asked before they began to read. Jeannie finished first. She leaned on me, looked up and smiled. Her head turned downward and I soon realized that she was reading the teacher's guide.

"Mr. Meyer," she whispered. "Is this what we are doing?"

"Well, yes," I said. "This book tells me what to do in the group."

She continued reading. "It tells you what to ask us. The questions are listed here," she said, incredulous. I think that she thought that I made up all those questions myself. I sensed her perception of me as all-knowing and incredibly brilliant was changing a bit. I moved my head to the side so I could see where Jeannie was focusing. Her eyes suddenly got very big.

"Mr. Meyer!" she whispered, quite excited now. "These are the answers!"

"Yes," I admitted. "They print those so teachers can be sure the kids say the right answer."

"Oh."

Others were finishing their reading and waiting, too. When the last child was about to finish, Jeannie turned to me and asked, "Can I do it?"

"Do what?" I asked.

"Can I ask the questions and see if they get them right?"

"Well, you have to be able to read this teachers guide," I said, knowing that she could do that quite easily.

"I can read it," she said.

"Well, okay," I said.

Jeannie proceeded to do the entire lesson. She told the group, via the guide, which pages to read, led them in locating answers in the text, directed them to pay close attention for certain details, and assigned the workbook pages. Sheepishly, I reached for the teacher's guide for the workbook and said to Jeannie, "Here, you might as well correct them when they are done, too."

Jeannie looked at the workbook I handed her. On the outside, it was the same as the one she had brought up to the group. She opened it and, for the second time this day, her eyes were huge. "These ... this ... it has the answers [printed] right in it!"

"Yes," I said. "That makes it easier for you to correct a lot of them quickly." And for the second time on the same day, I felt myself slip a notch on some scale Jeannie kept in her mind about me. But the truth was out and I wanted it all out.

The days that followed were remarkable. Different children in that group wanted to teach the group. They could read the guide and it struck me that they did not need the guide. They did not need that book or the stories or the skills it offered. As they were taking each other through the basal, I had more time to work with my other students, as I had promised I would.

Jeannie's group raced through the first half of the second-grade reading program in a matter of weeks. Then they wanted to do the second half, which they did. By February, they needed the third-grade pile.

But that was not allowed.

If they got too far ahead, what would happen in sixth grade? I was offered some older editions of a different second-grade basal, which I took. The children led the way, again. They wanted to read their library books and make up plays and do paintings about their reading. I suggested puppet shows and dioramas, and over the course of the months that followed, they invented a literature-based program.

The other reading groups wanted to do the same types of things. They wanted to teach themselves, and I found that with some assistance (or not) they could. I was a little humbled. After all, I had been too insecure upon completing my bachelor's degree to get a job, so I went right on through with a masters. Now, with this advanced degree, I found that I was not needed in any conventional capacity. The children were leading me in the redefinition of the reading program. They showed me that they already knew much of what they were expected to learn in second grade.

The children who had been lumped into one or the other of the two lower groups were a shock, too. They were not all the same. How could such a thing happen if the teachers covered the same material? I was pretty confused, but found that my confusion was more comfortable than ignoring what the kids could do. Luckily, as years passed, I found other teachers with similar stories, and together we supported our mutual growth as literacy educators. Most importantly, we paid attention to the children in our classroom. The children were the points of origin of curriculum in reading, and later in other subject areas. As we learned from our children and each other, we found subject areas overflowing into each other. We were empowering ourselves and our students.

My experience with Jeannie happened early in my teaching career, but paying attention to children was becoming an integral part of my teaching. This may have been a result of becoming more comfortable with classroom life and perhaps not feeling as though I needed to be in control. I was intuitively kid-watching (Goodman, 1985) and taking cues from my students as I began relying on them to show me how to teach.

THE S WORD

In the story of Leo, I learned that children typically intuit the range of voices, or registers (Halliday, 1975), possible or acceptable in a classroom context. Yet there are boundaries to acceptability that are blatantly or more subtly challenged by students and, in certain situations, teachers. One word can affect the nature of the relationship between teacher and student or teacher and teacher. Recall that Halliday described the nature of these relationships as their tenor. We rely on the tenor of relationships with others in deciding what to say and how to say it. We usually consider where we are (the field) and the type or mode we'll use (oral or written). Field, tenor, and mode form the frame I use to understand these stories about one word.

The nature of 'school talk' changes over time, yet some words remain unacceptable for a variety of reasons. Even though we might use certain words outside of the school situation, we often respond negatively when the words appear too near the school. Paul said *shit.* He said it a lot. He told other children they were full of it, he said some cafeteria food looked like it, he told kids that their heads were made of it, and he loudly exclaimed it if he struck out or was called out in various playground games.

It didn't bother me much. I grew up with the word, yet I would never say it within earshot of a teacher. There are some rules about language that I had intuited but Paul had not. I was unsure of what to do. What if a child went home and complained about Paul's use of it? Our principal was also a minister and he would not approve. Other kids might begin using the word. Other teachers suggested that I talk to Paul.

I had a long talk with him. My goal was to inform him about the use of language in school and at home. I told him that if he was allowed to use that word at home, he could continue to do so, but he had to stop using it in school. It was a bad word in school. He did know other bad words so he knew about words that were not appropriate for use in school. Other children would report, "Paul said the F word." He never used that word within a teacher's hearing range. I told him that the same rules applied to the S word as applied to the F word. I thought he understood.

It didn't stop.

We had another long talk and I said I would have to begin keeping him inside because his language offended other children and teachers on the playground. I explained that I much preferred that he go outside, and that I knew he preferred that as well. I would give him one more chance. It didn't work. He spent the next three recess times inside the classroom. It was sort of enjoyable for me, and perhaps also for him. We talked about a lot of things. He told me about his father who had his voice-box removed because he had cancer. He told me about heating with wood; I loved the smell of his clothing.

Each day, I reminded him of why he was indoors. Then we would talk, I would look at work the children had completed in the morning, then we would play a game or just chat. I liked it; I looked forward to it because he was teaching me so much about rural life. He talked about hunting and fishing and trapping. He told me about the spring behind his house where the family got their water. The 3-day sentence went by quickly and Paul was released to the playground.

His first day outside was a disaster. He had said the S word all over the playground, to kids, teachers, and even a dog passing by outside the playground fence. I had him remain inside the next day. I looked at him sternly. "Paul, do you understand why you are in here?"

"Yes."

There was a long pause. He did understand. I knew it and he knew it. I approached him and raised my hand slightly to put my arm around him. He jumped, apparently thinking that I was about to hit him. That told me a lot. I put my arm slowly down, around his back and hugged him gently. "Paul," I said. "Cut the shit."

Blood rushed to my face. I could feel it. I knew that if he ever told anyone that I said that I would be in, well, deep shit. He was quiet about it, although I did sweat for a few weeks. He also stopped using that word.

The shit did not stop there, though. Gracie, who lived in a log cabin her father and mother built with logs from their own land, also said it. She used it in the most clinical sense. She would come up to me on the playground and chat.

"We're planning on going to some place warm near the ocean this winter, Mr. Meyer," she said. "My dad and mom want a break from the cold and my little sister, Angie, needs some sun."

"That sounds great," I said. "Bring me back some seashells and some sunshine."

I was so pleased that she got to travel places and see things. She reported to us about her trips to Ottawa and even told us about her grandpa who had been paid to come from Europe to be the first doctor for a small town nearby. She had a rich life. I had met her parents when they invited my family to their home for a spaghetti dinner. They were honest, straightforward people who did not mince their words. They shared everything. Gracie had even seen Angie born, right in their home with a midwife present. She described it for us in detail and we were all amazed.

"My mom said that she had to take a shit, right in the middle of one of her contractions." (Gracie had also told us about contractions when I was teaching about a different sort of contraction in reading group.) Some children looked at me and I smiled and said to Gracie, "It must have been amazing to see a baby being born." I wanted the class to focus on what was important here, although I knew I was taking a risk with the S word.

One day on the playground, Gracie approached me. "I have to take a shit," she said. "May I please go inside?"

"Go on inside, Gracie," I said. "Oh, and Gracie, in school, we just say that we're going to use the restroom. You don't have to describe what you are going to do there."

"Oh, okay," she said. She never used the word in school again.

But that word would not go away. The contexts of our daily language lives saturate what we say, what we do, who we are, and how we express ourselves. Barb taught me that before I could articulate it.

Barb was the first-grade teacher, right next door to my second-grade room. One rather cold and icy morning, I stopped in the teacher's lounge and sat down for a cup of tea. Barb was white and shaking.

"What?" I asked. "What is it?"

She took a long drag of her cigarette. Her eyes filled and I thought she was going to cry. The sixth-grade teacher came into the teacher's lounge. He looked at her, looked at me, and then began laughing his deep belly laugh.

"What?"

"Tell him, Barb."

Her face had some color in it again and she smiled.

"We were coming to school this morning," she began, reminding me that she and the sixth-grade teacher took turns driving. "I was driving. We were near Maggie's house, so I could see far ahead."

The stretch of road she described was a familiar one. The windy mountain roads we traveled each winter day terrified me this time of year. The only flat straight section was close to 1 mile long and ran past the farm where Maggie and Frank, the gym teacher, live.

"The whole stretch was really icy. My car started to slide to the left, just as a school bus approached from the other direction."

The sixth-grade teacher could not contain himself any longer. He took over the telling of the story. "So, she points at the bus and screams, 'Look! Look! Bus! Bus! Shit! Shit!'" Barb sounded just like the basal stories she used with her first graders.

I've heard Ken Goodman tell a story like this about a first-grade teacher seeing a flat tire after a full day of school and saying something similar. But having heard this from Barb, with the help of the sixth-grade teacher, I thought it would fit in here, with the uses of shit in and near the school because, after all, the children are not the only ones to make decisions about the use of a register of language. Bloome's (1983) description of the social context of literacy processes applies here. The teacher, too, learns about language use in the classroom context. It is the text within the context. Barb had taught the basal reader to first graders for 20 years and now, at one of life's trying moments, she sounded like the language in which she had been emerged in the basal context.

I was learning to pay attention to language. Indeed, consistent with Halliday's (1988) findings, I was learning language, learning through language, and learning about language. By framing these stories in the professional literature about language and literacy, I found myself striving to make sense of why things happen the way they do, rather than trying to control, change, or make things the way I expect them to be. This does not mean I never offer input, but it usually results in watching and learning for longer periods before I intervene. It also means learning to find authentic opportunities to teach.

TAMI

Shirley Brice Heath (1983) also sensitized me to the relationship between language and culture. Describing her research, she explained that her work has "… been about how teachers' knowledge of children's ways with words enabled them to bring these ways into their classrooms" (p. 343). Schools seem, at times, to have a convoluted relationship with the communities they are serving. As we pay attention to the individuals in our classrooms, we want to know their stories. I wanted to know more about Tami's life outside of school to help make sense (for me) of her life within school.

Tami hated school. I suppose if this was not one of my first years of teaching I might have been more open to the idea of a student hating school, but Tami confused me. I was still new at teaching second grade and I wanted the children to love coming to school, to love seeing me each day as much as I loved seeing them. Tami hated school.

Quietly, at different times during the school day, Tami would disappear. I was overwhelmed with horror the first time it happened. I looked up from the group I was working with to scan the room and noticed her empty desk. I looked at the various centers and saw no one in any of the chairs there. I was shocked. I lost one. That does not look good for a new teacher, especially a male who wanted so desperately to teach a primary grade and wanted everything to be perfect.

I felt the blood drain out of my head and thought I would faint when I heard the sound of a chair moving in the far corner of the room. There was Tami. She had moved a desk and wriggled behind it and was seated on the floor in the corner. I asked her to please go back to her seat. She looked at me without saying a word and went back to her desk.

"I hate school," she said. I heard this as, "I hate you, Mr. Meyer." I felt so hurt. This was all so personal.

A few times each day, Tami would disappear and was usually found in that same spot. I grew a little more comfortable with it. I invited Tami to take some of her work with her when she went under the table, but she declined. Other children, hearing the invitation, decided to work in other places. Tami had helped to changed the work environment, although not intentionally. I began to get used to the idea of kids being comfortable when they worked and where they worked. I also started to study how they were working when they left their desks. I was a new teacher and didn't want to lose control (as if I ever had it).

Tami hated school. She would disappear to her private space but would not take any work with her. She just sat and sucked the index and middle fingers of her right hand at the same time. One day I decided to visit her under there. I contorted my body to squeeze next to her. She looked at me with disdain. I chatted with her; well, more accurately, I talked at her. I told her about learning and reading and all sorts of stuff she couldn't care about.

Each day she hid there, I made it my goal to visit with her. She never talked to me. Then, one day, Tami announced that she had some news. She went to the front of the room and told the kids that her father got a new bull and that it had a seed sack "this big," as she held her hands about 18 inches apart in the air. Many of the children made sounds of admiration. Tami looked at me. "I don't understand," I said.

Tami rolled her eyes. She looked at me and said, "You don't know what a seed sack is, do you, Mr. Meyer?" Now I hated myself for not knowing. I was raised in and near New York City. A seed sack. Wouldn't that be something you carry a seed in? Why would a bull need one? I shook my head no, telling Tami without words that I didn't know what it was. She laughed and laughed all the way back to her seat.

Maybe Tami did hate both school and me.

I went to the fifth-grade teacher who was becoming a friend. I asked him about a seed sack for a bull and he laughed at me. "Why do you ask?" he had to know. I explained about Tami. He knew her. There had been a lot of talk about her last year and it was decided she would be in my room this year. Gary told me what a seed sack was. It is the sack that contains the bull's testicles (his scrotum). Now what?

Tami hated school, but she must love something. I decided to stop at Tami's house on the way home from school to see the seed sack. I was truly curious about this thing. The school nurse told me where Tami lived and I stopped there about 1 hour after school was out.

I pulled into the driveway and, again, found myself in culture shock. I was a city kid who wanted to live in the country all his life. So here I was in the most rural part of New York state and loving what I was learning and also finding out that I didn't know very much at all. Tami lived on a farm. Her dad raised cows for milking for the local cheese factory. I beeped as I pulled into the driveway.

Tami's dad and her sister, Dana, whom I knew from the year before, greeted me. I had never met Tami and Dana's dad, so I shook hands with him and told him how proud Tami was of their farm. I told him that Tami had told me about the new bull and I asked him if he would allow her to show him to me. Tami's dad spit a big brown sticky thing from his mouth to the frozen ground. He smiled. His teeth were tobacco brown. He told Dana to "fetch Tami."

Tami approached me from the house that her father had built, in total disbelief. Her eyes were screaming, "What are you doing here?" I told her why I had stopped and that her dad had said it was okay for me to see the bull. She walked me to the barn. We went in and I was amazed at Tami's world. The barn was huge; it had a high ceiling, as barns do, but I had not been in one before. Tami showed me the bull. Dutifully, I walked around the side of the bull's pen so that I could see his sack. I looked at Tami and said, "That is big." She looked at me as though she expected something else to come from my mouth but I had no idea what to say.

"Mr. Meyer," she said, "Did you ever pull a calf?"

"Tami, I would never want to hurt a poor little calf by pulling it."

She laughed and laughed. As we walked back to the house, she told me that if a calf is being born but does not move out fast enough, a person would have to reach into the cow and pull the calf out. Sometimes, they tied bailing twine around the calf's feet to pull it out. Tami told me she had done that.

"Did she tell you she pulled a calf," her father asked as we entered the house.

"Yes," I said.

Tami's mother was taking a pork roast (a pig of their own they had recently slaughtered) from the oven and invited me to stay for dinner. I told her I had other plans but would love to come another day. I didn't have plans. I needed a rest from what I had seen. I needed to reflect on the day's events. I also wanted an excuse to come back another time. I would, eventually, come for supper.

Tami had pulled a calf. I tried to picture that in my mind. She was 8 years old. She sucked her fingers. She hated school and she pulled a calf.

I realized how little I knew about where I was teaching. I had my eyes on a piece of land, a lifelong dream, but I wasn't paying attention to life around me. So I started to ask Tami lots of questions about farming. I asked her about manure and how it gets taken out of the barn, and if she ate the animals she raised (she did). I asked her about growing corn and also learned about bulk tanks and electric fences ("Don't ever pee on one, Mr. Meyer"). Tami and I formed a relationship.

She still went under the desk to suck her fingers, and occasionally to work. But I became a visitor she could tolerate under there. I visited her there and at home and she taught me a lot. I thanked her a lot. I thanked her for every bit of information she gave me. She helped me talk to the other parents of the children in my class and to the other children, too. Tami taught me a lot about the language of that rural part of New York state. The rules there were very different than city living rules. She never became a lover of school, but she did become a credible and reliable resource. It was a role that made her important to me, and, through me, to others. I think she sensed her importance.

School became okay for Tami. I became okay for Tami. And she became okay for me. And I think it's okay to take teaching personally because my personal and professional lives overflow into each other. I was finding myself—finding that, in spite of my own education, I was a learner. The rural context in which I was teaching brought with it an urgency to learn in order to teach. I was inventing myself as a teacher in a context that was new to me in many ways. I was learning the children's ways with words.

NO WAY

This story is best framed in a theory of learning. A theory of learning and teaching is a powerful ally for a teacher. The *zone of proximal development* (Vygotsky, 1978) has become one way in which I make sense of teaching and learning. The zone is

> the distance between the actual developmental level as determined by independent problem solving and the level of potential development as determined through problem solving under adult guidance or in collaboration with more capable peers. (p. 86)

Qualitatively, the zone of proximal development suggests a sensitivity on the part of the teacher to know when he or she is contributing to children's opening of a zone. At such instances, saying or doing or providing something may support the children in their development. Learning to recognize such instances is something that requires a teacher to open a zone of proximal development as a teacher; indeed, the zone of proximal development is a mutual construction. It is a place where the ground is fertile for learning by the teacher and the student. Michael Cole (personal communication, October 1993) called teachers and students *covoyagers* as they engage in their mutual construction of the zone.

The zone of proximal development is not a metaphor for me. It is a real place and rests at the intersection of my background knowledge and the background knowledge of others with whom I am learning. We come together and, in some way, we present what we know. Sometimes that yields expected results, other times it does not.

The Electric Company (Children's Television Workshop) was a popular educational television show during the first few years I was teaching in rural New York state. Once each week, we would watch the show. Our school was small, on a very limited budget with few 'special classes' (art, music), and the teachers usually put a few classes together so that we could have some planning time while the children watched. I enjoyed this time because I got to know my colleagues and we could share some ideas as well as talk about children who concerned us. I realize now that I rarely watched the show.

One Friday, we put the two second-grade classrooms together to watch the show because it had been raining all week. This meant that we followed an indoor schedule resulting in no breaks or planning time for the teachers during the day. We decided that we would each take a 15-minute break during the show, with the other teacher remaining with both classes. I took the first break and, upon returning, I found a space on the floor near two second graders and watched the show with them. There we sat, in the foothills of the most remote mountain range of New York state, rain falling, leaves just about gone from the trees. I looked out the window and sort of got lost in the trees and streaks of rain tears running down the windowsill. I was brought back to the reality of my responsibilities when I heard many of the children saying, "Ohhhh, I like this part."

"Mee toooooo," others said.

I watched.

What followed was a medley of real street signs in Manhattan. I was born near New York City and spent many days there. Now, 400 miles away, I saw some familiar sights on the television screen. Street signs flashed on the screen, put to music: *one way, don't walk, walk, stop, no parking, danger, parking, restaurant, subway,* and more. Each sign was authentic, in its correct context, photographed from the city streets. The show ended shortly after that.

After the other teacher returned to claim her class, I talked to my kids about nostalgia. I told them that sometimes I missed the city because there was so much to do there, and I recollected some of my favorite restaurants. They began to talk about life in the city. Paul said he had been to a nearby town, which he called a city. He said his father hated it there because of all the traffic and pollution. That town has two traffic lights and is surrounded by farms. Paul taught me a lot about perspective and context.

I told the class that the signs made me think a lot about the city. I asked what signs they recalled seeing and I began listing them on the board. I put each sign in its appropriate shape. I drew the arrow for *one way* and tried to letter it the same way it was lettered on real streets. We had almost all the signs that were in the song, except one. I wrote *subway* on the board and said that this was the only other one I could remember. There was a silence and I asked who knew what a subway was.

Silence.

I explained that in New York City the streets and buildings take up so much room that it made sense to build a train system beneath the surface of the city. That way, cars and trucks and buses could move along the surface and trains could move many people below the surface as well.

More silence.

They didn't believe me. They had on their faces the same expression I had seen on Theresa's face when she came to me with a word she did not know. She had taken a book out of the library and was reading about different kinds of birds and came across the word *flamingo*. I explained that it was a tall pink bird that usually stood on one leg with its beak in the water. She looked at me and said, "Nah." I tried to convince her, even went to the library and found a book with a picture, yet she still looked at me as though I had told her that this bird drove a motorcycle. She had never seen such a bird and would have no part of my explanation.

So it was with the subway. I tried to explain and re-explain and told how I would travel from Chinatown to The Museum of Natural History by taking the subway. No, they were having no part of it. I told the class about the Metropolitan Transit Authority (MTA) and I said that I would write to them to ask if there were movies of the subway for me to show them—proof that such trains existed.

It took about 3 weeks, but the MTA responded by sending a promotional film about the subway system. It must have been made in the late 1940s, which made it seem more like a horror movie. I kept waiting for giant lizards to appear. The film showed a businessman carrying a very important looking briefcase as he walked down a busy city street. He approached the familiar green fence (although it was dark gray in this black and white film) that surrounded the stairway down to the subway. We saw the man walking down the stairs. I turned the sound off and explained to the kids what was happening. He was descending below the level of the street to get a train.

The next scene was from in front of the man. Our point of view was from below the ground as the man was descending the stairs and walking toward us. He was underground. He approached the token booth, purchased a token, and proceeded through the turnstile to the platform. We could see the tracks as the camera focused beyond the man. Then, the camera turned toward the dark tunnel. "You see," I said, "he is underground and it's dark. The train will come through that tunnel. We can see the man because there are lots of lights down there. But there are few lights in the tunnels. The trains are well lit, though."

Finally, there was a light from deep within the tunnel. The subway train was coming closer. It pulled up to the platform, the man got on, the door closed, and the camera turned to follow the train disappearing down the continuation of the tunnel to its next stop.

I stopped the film and asked the class what they thought.

"It's nice," said Linda.

"Yes," said Paul. "But it wasn't underground. Trains can't go underground. They're too big. We see trains on our way to town, so they're not underground."

"But …" I began. "Well, look, I'll run the film backwards."

The class was genuinely shocked. Their first grade teacher showed them some movies both in forward and reverse and they were greatly incensed when I refused to do the same. Now, I was doing what I said I would never do.

"You see, " I continued, "the train had picked him up. Now it's coming and he's getting off … well really on but this is in reverse and look …" I continued my narration as the man walked backward through the turnstile, past the token booth, and up the stairs, facing down.

"You see, now, he's coming up. He had gone underground to get the train."

They were having none of it.

"It's a good movie, Mr. Meyer. Show it again," one of the children suggested.

I knew that few in the class believed that a subway could do what it indeed did do each day of the year. I asked about their families and their vacations and where they had been. "What's the farthest you've ever been from your home?" The children spoke of the lake or the pond as places where they would spend a weekend. Many spoke of hunting lodges and camps. I tried to get a sense of the farthest that they had ever been from this part of New York. Well, there was that busy town nearby that has two traffic lights. …

Were these kids so different from the ones I had met in the Head Start program in New York City a few years ago? The contexts were different, as different as they could get, yet their construction of what was real and what was possible was saturated with the social fabric into which their lives were woven. When I write their stories—my stories of my life with them—I learn about them and myself.

(That was another invitation to write. Now, are you writing?)

HOME AND SCHOOL

The relationship between the home and the school was described and analyzed by a variety of researchers (Clay, 1987; Emig, 1971). In 1932, Willard Waller wrote:

> From the ideal point of view, parents and teachers have much in common, in that both, supposedly, wish things to occur for the best interests of the child; but, in fact, parents and teachers usually live in a condition of mutual distrust and enmity. Both wish the child well but it is such a different kind of well that conflict must inevitably arise over it. The fact seems to be that parents and teachers are natural enemies, predestined each for the discomfiture of the other. The chasm is frequently covered over, for neither parents nor teachers wish to admit to themselves the uncomfortable implications of their animosity, but on occasion it can make itself clear enough. (p. 68)

Rather than point a blaming finger at a child's home or involve myself in ways that cultivate the 'discomfiture' Waller described, I write the stories of my experiences with children's out-of-school lives in order to gain insights into those lives, in order to make my classroom a more real place for the children, and in order to understand where it is that the members of the class are in their journeys as learners. As I visited more and more homes, I found each one unique and, of course, deeply impactful on children's lives in school.

Reading about home–school relationships is not always comfortable. Annette Lareau (1989) wrote candidly about the differences between the school experiences of higher and lower socioeconomic groups. Her writing helped me understand some of my experiences. I wish I had read work like hers while I was teaching and that I had a strong support group to help make sense of it. The stories we (you and I) write can teach us because, as we write and think, we make sense of our students' lives and our teaching lives. By increasing our understanding, the animosity to which Waller referred can disperse leaving us clearer in our understanding of who we are and what we are teaching.

SHARON

Notes from home could probably fill a book and would teach us much about the use of written language in the community. Does spelling count in notes from home? Some parents imposed their own rules about the use or acceptability of conventional spelling. One of my favorites came from Mrs. D the day after her daughter had been absent. A transcription follows:

> Dear Mr. Meyer,
> Sharon was absent on Feb. 4
> because she had ~~the dri~~e
> ~~djerve djahr~~ the runs.
>
> Sincerely,
> Mrs. D

Now that's a short story. It's important because it shows that we can be like anthropologists as we gather the evidence that supports our stories. We can collect artifacts from our lives as teachers and use the artifacts to stimulate discussion, gain insights, and learn about our students and their lives.

DAVID

Some families did not seem concerned with how their homes were viewed by the school. Visiting these homes provided me with insights into the fabric into which children would weave their learning.

David taught me a lot about the way my students live because his was one of the first homes I visited. Once I was a classroom teacher in this rural district, I decided that home visitation was an integral part of the program and tried to visit the home of every student at least once. I had given this idea lip service in September, but it was November and I still had not visited one home. I passed many of the children in my class as they waited for the school bus in the morning. I knew where David lived; I had passed his house on the way to and from school each day and had admired the stone chimney that was built on the side of the house.

David told me in early November that he would have to have his tonsils removed. I was surprised as he was not particularly sickly and had not missed much school. I didn't think he was having ear infections. The class wanted to make him cards and I volunteered to visit him to deliver the cards and drop off some books for him to read while he recuperated. I knew David's family heated with wood because of the amount of smoke which billowed from the chimney, and assumed the house was warm inside.

I approached the house noticing the worn white clapboards and walked up the wooden stairway that led to the front door. I knocked and when his mom (I assumed the woman answering to be his mom) answered the door, I explained who I was. She invited me in. I stepped up the last wooden step and realized that I expected to enter onto a floor that was level with the door opening but that instead I needed to step down once through the doorway because David's house had a dirt floor. It was my first home visit and I was clearly in a state of culture shock. The beautiful stone chimney did not show on the inside; all that could be seen was a large cookstove sending a lot of heat into the room. It was over 90°F in the house and I began to sweat. Wood heat is hot and it is dry. The air dried my nose. I felt sorry for David as I thought of the sore throat he must already have from the surgery, now aggravated by the hot, dry air.

There were about five adults present and I smiled at all and explained who I was. No one introduced themselves as David's parents. They all nodded at me. I looked for David. He was in a chair in the far corner of the large room. His entire head was shaved. His eyes were big and they were red as though he had been crying or perhaps some smoke escaped into the room when the stove was being stoked. This was a common occurrence and many of the children in my class smelled like wood smoke all winter long.

I said to the woman who had answered the door that I was surprised David's head had to be shaved to have his tonsils removed. She said that the hospital had not touched his hair. He had come home from the hospital just the day before and was served a bacon sandwich as his first meal at home. He had complained because the bacon hurt his throat and refused to eat it. His father said to eat it or he would be punished and David had refused again. As punishment for his disobedience, David's father had shaved his head.

I am not the hero type. I never seem to know what to say until I am driving away. I went over to where David sat and gave him the tan envelope containing get well wishes from his classmates. Then I explained to him that I had brought him some books to read and that he could return them when he was back in school. I felt the eyes of all the adults on my back and felt myself turning red from heat and anger. I told him I hoped we would see him soon and turned to the woman who had let me in and thanked her. I left. Driving home, I could not think of something to say. I had no face to which to address my anger—I did not know which of the men in the room was his father. As I sat in my apartment that evening, I still saw the flames that could be seen through the cracks in the wood burning stove at David's house. I could see the dirt floor there and the oak in the rooms I rented. I remember wondering just what it was that I could teach David. What would make sense? He had changed me. His family had changed me. His tonsils had changed me.

When I took a human relations course from David and Virginia Aspy, they taught us listening techniques. One of the techniques was a physical exercise in which we positioned ourselves in a chair ready to receive what a speaker was saying. We were told to lean forward and hold our hands as though we were receiving an egg; we had to make sure our hands 'said' "I will hold all that you offer both firmly and safely." Robert taught me to try to hold lives that way when they are presented to us as teachers. Firmness and safety of hold demands respect and the mutual construction of an environment and curriculum.

I told the class that I had stopped and dropped off the cards and thought David would be happy to be back in school. I told them I missed him a lot, which was not originally true. I missed him—but not a lot. He had been a kid that quietly blended in. I had been a kid that quietly blended in. When he returned to school, his hair was 'fuzzy'' and no one said anything about it.

Children like David taught me that children need to be stars for more than 15 minutes in their lifetimes. They need to be stars every day. Even now, as I write this, he evokes in me a sadness from a deep, deep place. I do not wonder about what school must be for children—I know what it must be. David's life at home could not cripple me in school; it inspired me to cultivate my love, my understanding, my willingness to look hard at what the children in the class have to offer and the power of what we must create together.

Writing his story is important because it is writing my story; it is me coming to terms with how I responded to a situation. It is a thoughtful process and I find myself learning as I write, reread, and rewrite. Do you have a David? Is there an intense story that has shaped you as a teacher? Are you writing yet?

A THOUGHT ON REVISION

One of the hardest things for me to do as I began to take myself seriously as a writer was to sit down with a piece and revise it. When I crossed out a single word, I felt as though I was slicing my own skin; moving a sentence was as fathomable as removing fingers from one hand and putting them on the other. These things just weren't done. After all, wasn't the piece just perfect as it rolled out of my brain, down my arm, and onto the paper? It just didn't seem to feel like I was writing when I was revising.

This all changed when I began to write with a word processor on a computer. I could save the original piece as one document and save subsequent versions as different documents. I could cut and paste and move things around quite a bit—without retyping. I began to look for themes that appeared in different sections of a piece and then group all of those themed paragraphs into the same section. My writing changed from a stream of consciousness that I considered a finished piece, to a stream of consciousness that was captured as raw material that could be worked with. I could shape the original piece, adding bits here, deleting parts, and moving others.

Now, I like to print out the first draft and mark it up like crazy. This gives me time away from my computer; time to play with my ideas and then return to the computer to enter those as a new version, saving each precious previous version. I've also become brave about dumping older versions. I do keep the hard copies, but I suppose I will eventually start to recycle that paper, too. Revision is a part of the writing process that can be enjoyable. It requires time and invention. You need the time to do it, and you need to be inventive about how you do it, so that it feels like the important work it is.

If you are hesitant to revise your work, I have one suggestion: Read it aloud. Most of us do not do this. As you read the piece aloud, you will find the parts that don't work. I find that reading pieces orally inspires revision. See if that works for you. Or, you could ask a very trusted colleague or friend to read a piece, but be sure to find a gentle reader. A writer's nightmare (for this writer) is receiving my own piece back from a reader only to find it murdered by slices, stabs, and punctures reminiscent of an English teacher who none of us want.

CLOSING THOUGHTS ON SHORT STORIES

The short stories I write and tell inevitably become part of the text and context of my graduate and undergraduate classes and of the teacher support group to which I belong. I tell stories to initiate or complement our ongoing conversations. Many times, these stories are springboards for our discussions about our live experiences in classrooms as learners and teachers.

I find myself, as a new member of higher education, encouraging teachers and future teachers to engage in research (Cochran-Smith & Lytle, 1990) because I am convinced that good teaching is research. Teaching has, at its core, inquiry. Teachers who are making the commitment to keep journals and systematically think about their practices and the activity in their classrooms are continually amazed at what they find out about themselves and the children. Mary Hinkley, a first-grade teacher reflecting in her journal about life in her classroom, wrote, "I want my classroom to be a safe place to think." She wants a thinking classroom for herself and her children.

Research once frightened my students. Now they know that research is stories. Now they are anxious to engage in understanding who they are as literate individuals and the impact of that understanding on their teaching and the learning that occurs in their classrooms. They have come to find that narrative expression is valuable; life is a story we live and one we can periodically stop and retell and analyze. Some of the stories from my past are like a warm bath (yes, I encourage the use of metaphor for teachers researching); my stories are something into which I can slip easily, are an important place to relax and reflect, and typically leave me refreshed and invigorated about what it is I do. I encourage you to save and savor your stories, to write and share them, because they are such a powerful point of origin for teacher growth.

When all is said and done, it seems that stories remain. After all the research, the hours in the library, the decisions we make as educators, the courses we take, the hours at meetings with parents or colleagues, the time we spend at our district office, and more—after all that, we return to our stories. Sylvia Ashton-Warner (1971) wrote her story as a teacher, A.S. Neil (1960) wrote his story of the children at a school he started, and many others have written theirs or are writing them now. Our stories remain. We pass them on gently, like eggs. Our heads are full of them and we need each other to validate them as part of what it means to study who we are and how we are growing. So, write your stories—in order to be an "abiding student of education," to break out of the "routine details," and to be moved by your own "independent intelligence"(Dewey, 1904, p. 107).

CHAPTER PERMISSIONS

The poem *Aunt Sue's Stories* first appeared in *Crisis Magazine,* 1921, p. 121. It is reproduced with permission of the publishers.

An earlier version of this chapter appears as "Stories to Teach and Teaching to Story" in *Language Arts* (April 1995), published by the National Council of Teachers of English.

chapter 3

Longer Stories

I was neither a good listener nor an able storyteller when my name became Teacher ... I was a stranger in the classroom, grown distant from the thinking of children.
—Paley (1990, p. 14)

Writing longer stories involves being a good listener and a good storyteller and committing oneself to getting closer to 'the thinking of children.' Longer stories take more time to write because they involve collecting "evidence" to include in the story. Framing the story involves reading other people's work (see chap. 5), and the thinking and subsequent physical acts of writing, rereading, and revising may turn into what seems like an endless loop. The reward for writing longer stories is that we learn so much from them. We learn, as Vivian Paley did in her stories about children, about ourselves and the children we teach. Writing longer stories brings us closer to the "thinking of children."

Writing longer stories requires passion, commitment, and motivation to act. Passion, in this context, means feeling deeply about some facet of our life as a teacher; we may feel passionate about a student or group or activity within our classrooms. Tom Romano (1994) wrote of passion:

> Passion causes ideas, images and lines of thought to stick with you throughout the day as you shop, exercise, prepare a meal or garden. Passion raises you from bed to jot down a phrase or a line you thought of as you were drifting to sleep. (p. 50)

Commitment involves time and choice; we choose to invest the time required to make sense out of something we feel passionate about and to put it in writing. Usually, passion and commitment motivate us to act. 'Acting' means taking the time to collect the pieces of the story, reading what others have written (or hearing what others have to say), and doing the writing. Longer stories tell of ongoing activities and experiences as they unfold, rather than the aspects of our teaching lives that are "occasional visits."

Longer stories involve the collection of evidence. We look for discussions and conversations in the classroom and tape record them or transcribe them verbatim. We might collect samples of writing, tapes of children reading, videotapes, audiotapes, science activities, and our own recollections and reflections in journals, on tapes, or in a computer. We collect because of our fascination, our commitment, our passion, and our motivation. A longer story unfolds over time; typically it is told and retold as we gather more information and increase our understanding of what is occurring within the story.

In this chapter, there are two long stories. The first one I collected and wrote with a kindergarten child. The second one was written by Kara, a fourth-grade teacher, telling the story of Robert. The stories are different, but they are supported by the assumption that collecting the stories, framing them, writing and rewriting them, and sharing them with caring and honest colleagues is a forum for one of the most profoundly powerful ways of professional growth.

CHOOSING A STORY AND STARTING TO WRITE

There are many stories to tell and choosing one as a focus is difficult. A long story is a commitment that will involve time: writing, in the library, reading, rewriting, and hours of thinking and analysis. Once you make a decision about which story to tell, you might find that, as the school year or other arbitrary period of time unfolds, you want to change your focus. There is nothing wrong with that. In your story, you can report the entire journey that you took. You can tell about beginning, changing your focus, refocusing that focus, and taking sidetrips as you become interested in things related to the major thrust of the story. The process of your interest as it develops and changes is a part of the story.

Next, you begin to collect the story. Researchers call this *collecting evidence*—so do detectives! We do it for the same reason: We want to convince the readers (judges) that the points we make are justified. You need to decide how to collect and store evidence over time. You might develop a filing system, or use a notebook with various types of dividers, or rely on a computer as a way to store and sort evidence. Audiotapes, videotapes, writing samples, science projects, math activities, photos, art projects, and songs may become part of your collection. The stories in this chapter use a variety of evidence and the collection and subsequent analysis of the data is discussed as part of each story.

Analysis is not easy. We read and reread the evidence we gather and make decisions about how to organize it. The intensity of work inherent in data analysis is often hidden because a story might seem to flow so smoothly. That is the sign of a good story. When we analyze data we look for patterns and themes that organize what we have collected. James Spradley (1980) wrote a book for anthropologists that taught me a lot about data analysis. Spradley reminded me to focus on "[1] what people do, [2] what people know, and [3] the things people make and use" (p. 5). In my analyses, I constantly keep these three broad areas in mind. I also decide which evidence will demonstrate for a reader what children are doing, what they know, and what they are making and using. Following the analysis, the data is presented in some form (oral, written, a display, etc.).

Let's turn, now, to the two stories in this chapter. They are two different demonstrations of possible ways for you to collect, analyze and write your longer stories.

ZOE

Zoe is my daughter. I have two children, 4 years apart, both girls. The older one, Sadie, is a curious, sensitive, and very literate person. Before I knew it, she was in first grade and busy reading and writing. This surprised me. I wondered how it happened so fast! Sadie's mom and I read many, many books to Sadie. We bought books and used the library to find more to enrich her literate life, but it seemed that all of a sudden she was reading and writing. As a second-grade teacher, I agreed with Ken Goodman (1986) that learning to read and write are natural processes, but I hadn't paid close enough attention to Sadie to learn about those processes. I was particularly interested in written language.

When Zoe was a few weeks old and Sadie was busy writing signs about Zoe's birth and making posters for Zoe's room, I made a parental mental note: Pay attention to Zoe's written language. When will it start? How will I know? My question for a longer story was thus chosen. I didn't think I was a researcher, but I was. I was a researcher in the field, like an anthropologist. My fields were parenthood and teaching.

Zoe grew and my wife and I marveled as our second daughter learned to speak. Zoe started her schooling experience at a program for 3-year-olds in the same school where I was teaching second grade. We had fun riding to school together and I periodically had time to visit her in her classroom. At home, Zoe drew pictures for her first teacher, Mrs. Fisher, using markers, crayons, and pencils. Mrs. Fisher received these with much excitement.

One day at home, after school, Zoe seemed to be working on another piece for her teacher. She was attentively hunched over a sheet of writing paper that came from my classroom. She showed it to me when she was done and said, "Daddy, read this."

I looked at her, "What do you mean?" I asked.

"It's a letter to my teacher."

Bells went off in my head. This was the first thing she had put on paper that she called writing. It was a moment I had awaited since her birth.

"What does it say?" she asked again.

"Ummm," I hesitated. What if I read it wrong? Could I just make up anything?

"My, ummm, my glasses are kind of dirty. Could you read it?" I asked.

FIG. 3.1. *Letter:* Dear Teacher, I hope you will come over. I hope you write back. You will see the tree house. Love Zoe.

"Okay," she said as she took the paper back. She read the letter, "Dear Teacher, I hope you will come over. I hope you write back. You will see the tree house. Love, Zoe."

You may wonder how a 3-year-old could write such a rich and interesting letter to her teacher. The letter has a salutation, a body, and a closing, just as you would expect in a letter. It has clear purposes: the desire for the teacher to visit Zoe's home, the desire for a response, and an enticement (You will see the tree house). Zoe demonstrates how much she understands about written language. Figure 3.1 shows Zoe's letter to her teacher.

The letter lacks conventional spelling, perhaps, but I would suggest that conventional spelling is all that it lacks. Zoe brought the letter to her teacher, read it to her, and requested that the teacher respond, which the teacher did.

As the year continued, Zoe wrote infrequently. Each piece that she wrote, I placed in a folder. I was collecting evidence. If she wrote something she wanted to mail or give to someone, I made a photocopy. On the back of each piece, in small writing, I wrote what the piece said in conventional spelling. The following year, as a 4-year-old, Zoe played with print quite a bit. She learned to write her name because her sister liked to spell it for her, wrote more letters to people, wrote a newspaper, and made cards and posters.

Framing My Understanding of Zoe's Writing

Making sense of Zoe's growth as a writer led me to what I call the *voices of outside experts.* I wanted to understand the information that is available about young writers, so I turned to the library for help. I began to read about written language development in school and home settings. My passion and commitment motivated me to learn more.

Books I Read as a Teacher.   I was not going into my research blind. I had taught second grade for 15 years and considered myself fairly current on the teaching of writing. As a teacher of primary-age children, I had read Don Graves (1983), Nancie Atwell (1987), and Lucy Calkins (1986). Calkins' book about one young writer (1983) made a strong impact on my thinking. This book is a case study of Susie, a second-grade student. Lucy asked Susie many of the questions I had for Zoe: Why are you writing this? What if you can't spell a word? Who supports you as a writer? Although these questions were not put to Susie or to Zoe directly, they were some of the questions Lucy and I asked of the written language activity we observed.

Thomas Newkirk's (1989) work excited me because he showed how children have many interests in and, therefore, many uses for written language. They don't just write stories. Their use of written language is as varied as that of adults who write all types of lists, fill out forms, write checks, leave quick notes, write longer letters, and much more.

I also attended conferences such as the local International Reading Association conference and the Whole Language Umbrella conferences, locally and nationally. The presentations and book sales at the conferences also provided me with ideas about which books to read. If you are truly passionate, motivated, and committed about something, you will probably find yourself reading, talking, thinking, and seeking other experiences (like conferences) that support and cultivate your interest.

Books I Read as a Parent.   I read Marie Clay's books (1984, 1987) because, quite honestly, they are easy to read. These skinny books took less than an afternoon to read and are full of children's writing that she explained as evidence of growth and development. Her findings and the things I was seeing in Zoe's writing were similar. Children are active users of written language.

In *Writing Begins at Home,* Clay cited a book by Glenda Bissex (1980). For the first time in my life, I looked at an author's references with the intention of finding more information. Bissex's book is about her son, Paul, and the reading and writing that he does at home and in school. The book is a comparison similar to the one I was involved in as I learned about Zoe.

Yetta Goodman, in one of many discussions we had about home and school, reminded me that Piaget studied his own children. Suddenly my work seemed very important! I also found other parents studying their kids' literacy. Mary Hill (1989), Michael Halliday (1975), and Judith Schickendanz (1990) studied their kids. The study of individual cases of children's literacy lives was justified for me within the literature on literacy.

Books I Read as a Researcher.   I believe that I was a researcher from the moment I decided to pay attention to Zoe's development as a writer. So, when you decide to pay attention to something as it grows and changes over time, you are a researcher. Teacher-researchers are increasing in numbers (Cochran-Smith & Lytle, 1993). As a graduate student, I focused on research methods, and also in greater depth on learning about written language development.

My learning about written language is best summarized by an "other voice," that of first-grade teacher and researcher, Mary Ellen Giaccobe (1986):

> Learners need time, choice, and response. I do not think teachers need to choose between learning to write or writing to learn. A productive classroom in any subject should provide opportunities for the student to wonder, to pose questions, to pursue possible answers, to discuss with others, to come to some conclusions—all in writing and all in an attempt to come to a greater understanding of what they are trying to learn. The research done by Graves and Calkins and Sowers, and by teachers experimenting with writing workshops in their classes, indicates … that writing can be the vehicle for learning—for learning about writing and for learning about particular topics in content areas. (p. 147)

Writers need the time to write, the opportunity to choose what they write (in topic, form, and function), and they need responses from caring audiences before and after making their work public.

Jane Hansen (1987) taught me that writers live and work in communities and that writing is a social activity. Writing is social because it shows itself in relationships and social situations, is the result of social situations, and is meant to affect social situations. Zoe writes in response to her world acting upon her and because she wishes to act upon her world. That is why any writer writes. This seems obvious, but the nature of the social situation is so important in Zoe's life as a writer. You will see, as I present her writing, how specific situations affect her writing activity.

Although the reading I did is important to me, it is not necessary to reiterate it here. I love to read others' work about written language. I encourage graduate students to read and write about the students in their elementary and middle-school classrooms. Find what provokes your curiosity and follow it until something more interesting comes along. That 'next something that comes along' does two things: It lets me know I am finished, perhaps temporarily, with one area, and leads me further into something new to learn about.

Making Decisions as a Researcher

Although I collected Zoe's writing when she was 3 and 4 years old, it wasn't until she entered kindergarten that her written language activity noticeably increased in quantity and quality. I also noticed a big difference between the types of writing she did at home and in school. School, once she entered kindergarten, became formal. There was a writing center and, when Zoe was assigned to work there, she was required to write certain things in certain ways. The spontaneity and choice that she was afforded earlier was gone.

The dramatic differences between home, where writing was still playful and centered around Zoe's interest, and school, where it had become systematic, led me to study the differences between home and school writing. Such differences do not make one place good and the other place bad. School is quite complex, with many children in one classroom and a teacher responsible for managing it. I wanted to understand how the two settings complemented each other, as evidenced in what Zoe learned over time. There was, then, a subtle shift in my interest. Rather than studying her writing development as one big "thing," I began to explore how the two settings contributed to her growth as a writer. In this chapter, I present only Zoe's growth in kindergarten. I already discussed her prekindergarten years, and continue to collect her writing today as she enters sixth grade. I limit myself to her kindergarten year to demonstrate one way of telling the story of 1 year's growth.

The sections that follow are about Zoe as a writer at home and then at school during kindergarten. I took one side trip while learning about Zoe's writing. I became intrigued with what children say when they are writing. The social activity in which Zoe was involved while she wrote expressed itself in what she said as well as in her writing (Dyson, 1993). Here, then, is my daughter, Zoe.

Zoe's Writing at Home

Zoe understood and could discuss the types of writing she used at home. She would say, "This is a note for you, Mom," or, "I am writing a story, now." Because she had names for the type of writing she completed at home, I use her categories in the sections to follow. When we tell our stories, we may decide to put our findings into categories. Sometimes the categories come right from the person or situation we are studying. For example, Zoe knew when she wrote a list, would call it a list, and, as I worked to make sense of her written language development, I used her category of *list*.

Zoe was (and remains) a coresearcher on this project. It's exciting to include those whom we are studying as coresearchers because they feel important and involved in the study. I ask her questions about her writing as we review what she has written. She offers insights, asks me what I think, and we engage in discussions about language. She becomes a language scientist with me. She decides if things can be shared with larger audiences. Zoe gave me permission to share her writing with you.

The categories that follow are about Zoe's writing at home. She chose the names of the categories by telling me how the written activity functioned. By listening to Zoe, I learned how she was organizing written language. These categories, and their frequency of use, fascinated me because they were so different across the home and school settings. Zoe's invented spelling patterns were similar across settings, but the different uses or functions of writing were so salient that I studied those in greater depth. The categories are presented in the sections to follow.

Writing Notes and Letters. Zoe wrote 15 notes and letters at home during the year. Figure 3.2 shows a quick note she wrote to her mom. It says, "Check my room quick. Hurry, it's almost clean." The note was written during the family's weekly clean up day. She wrote the note quickly and received what she had requested: Her mom checked Zoe's cleanup progress. Zoe knew that notes got the attention of family members and could result in a break from the work at hand. I am sure she relied on my fascination with her writing as a vehicle for derailing boring chores.

I received a note, one that was more typical in that Zoe used conventional letters, when I arrived home from class one evening. Figure 3.3 is a sticky note, a popular writing medium at our house, that was placed on the kitchen table. The note refers to our dog, Bo, who had an accident on a rug. The note lays out the important message and shows the rug where the deed was done.

She handed notes to her mom after her mom answered the phone (Fig. 3.4) asking "Who is it?" Figure 3.5 shows a note Zoe wrote to herself. She found and wore a button that said, "Can you read?" and copied it onto a sticky note. Then she wrote, "Yes, I can," and wore that on her shirt.

FIG. 3.2. *Note:* Check my room quick. Hurry, it's almost clean.

FIG. 3.3. *Note:* Dad, Bo was bad.

FIG. 3.4.   *Note*: Who is it?

FIG. 3.5.   *Note*: Can you read? Yes, I can.

Zoe wrote a note to her mom requesting that they go to the bakery and take Zoe's friend, Monica, too (Fig. 3.6). She wrote, "Monica wants to come to the bakery with us," and handed her mom the note. Mom was in the middle of a discussion with other adults, including Monica's mom, and Zoe did not want to interrupt. Writing was a way to make her wishes known and to circumvent the norms of courtesy.

FIG. 3.6. *Note:* Monica wants to come to the bakery with us.

I realize that I am including many notes, but I found them so interesting that I had difficulty limiting myself to the ones presented here. The final one is fascinating because it implies, "Hey, look what I can do." It is a note to her mom that reads, "To mom," and then lists the alphabet and ends with two kisses and two hugs (Fig. 3.7). Zoe used some upper case letters and some lower case ones. I venture to guess that she used lower case e because she learned to use that in her name. Clay (1984) explained that children sometimes write to do a sort of inventory of what they know. Perhaps Zoe was sharing such an inventory of her knowledge of the alphabet with her mom.

Zoe delighted in the attention that her notes brought on her, just as a baby learning to speak delights in the attention and subsequent action brought by her first words. This young writer continues to love making herself known and heard in her world by using written language.

Authoring Stories.   Zoe wrote seven stories at home during the year. She typically made an announcement such as, "I'm going to write a story now," and she would work at the kitchen table or in her room. During some stories, anyone in earshot would hear, "How do you spell ..." and she would request a word. More often, she would write the story with no assistance and then read it to those around her. Figure 3.8 shows one of Zoe's stories about a kid who urinated on the floor because he could not find the bathroom in school. This was written near the

FIG. 3.7.   The letters of the alphabet, kisses, and hugs.

beginning of the school year and is not a true story. Perhaps it reflects her own fear of not finding the bathroom and being embarrassed in front of her colleagues in kindergarten.

Zoe's favorite book during the autumn of her kindergarten year was *Are You My Mother?* (Eastman, 1960). She used words she could find and read from that book to write the story shown in Fig. 3.9. Zoe wrote the date at the top of the page because she had seen me putting dates on her work. The story says, "I am a cat. This is a bird. My name is Nel." Nellie is Zoe's middle name; she likes to be called Nel or Nellie from time to time. The story shows her use of a dash because the word *name*

FIG. 3.8. *Story:* PU, a kid peed. Yuck.

FIG. 3.9. *Story:* I am a cat. This is a bird. My name is Nel.

did not fit on one line. Where did she learn that? "I don't know, I just know it," she said. How fascinating! When does a child learn to use a dash like this? The more she wrote, the more I came to believe that we may continually underestimate young writers.

Making Lists.   Zoe loves to write lists because our family is a family of list writers. We write grocery lists, gift lists, party lists, and more. Our grocery list is typically written in a small spiral-bound notebook. Zoe's first participation is shown in Fig. 3.10. She added to the list: brownies and chocolate chip cookies. You can see her understanding of some of the correspondence between letters and sounds in the word *brownies. Chocolate chips* has got to be long because it sounds like so many words or syllables, so she made it long.

Another type of list she wrote during the year is one that helps organize others. This is a unique use of list writing in that no family member had ever used lists to organize family activity before. Figure 3.11 shows the list of chores that Zoe assigned me. As you may recall, our dog's name is Bo. During one of our Saturday clean-the-house days, Zoe called from her room, "How do you spell chores?"

Sadie answered, knowing well the routine that one letter is called at a time until a signal is given to go on to the next letter.

"C," Sadie called out.

"Okay," came the voice from Zoe's room.

"H."

"Okay."

"O." The calling of letters goes on until the word is spelled in its entirety. The quiet that followed led me to believe that Zoe had written the word and was back

FIG. 3.10.   *Items on a grocery list:* brownies *and* chocolate chip cookies.

FIG. 3.11. *Items on a list of chores:* Chores for Dad: clean toilets; do a few dishes; Bo poop.

to cleaning her room. In a few minutes, she emerged from her bedroom with the list, (Fig. 3.11), showing my assigned tasks (Chores for Dad: clean toilets; do a few dishes; Bo poop [meaning I need to clean the backyard]).

Zoe asked for help with the first word, but invented spelling for the remainder of the list. A close look shows that she has conventionally spelled many parts of the words in her list, such as the *oo* in *poop.*

Just as important as the convention of spelling is her demonstration of an understanding for a use of lists. Lists organize our lives and Zoe is very willing to use them to organize the lives of others. I suggested that she make a list of what she was going to clean up and she rolled her eyes, "Ohhh, Dad." It seems that this use of list writing is specific to others. She established a precedent in the family. We now regularly use lists during days that we clean; we list the jobs and family members choose the ones they will do.

Producing Signs.   Zoe made six signs during the year. She put up signs for the stores and restaurants she opened with her sister or friends. One of the sadder signs she wrote during the year was one that marked the grave of her invisible friend. On a large sticky note, she wrote, "Grave, do not sit," and placed the sign near our small flower garden (Fig. 3.12).

FIG. 3.12.   *Sign:* Grave: Do not sit.

FIG. 3.13.   *Sign announcing that a child is lost.*

As a parent who panics easily, I wondered if we needed to start therapy because of this death. Her invisible friend reappeared (to her) a few days later, much to my relief.

Zoe made two signs when Lana's mother called asking if Sadie had seen Lana (Sadie's friend). Sadie had not seen her, nor had anyone else in our family. Zoe got two sheets of paper and made two 'lost kid' signs (Fig. 3.13). She went outside and hung one on the mailbox and the other on the garage door. Kathy Short (1992) would refer to this as *intertextuality,* because the text of our milk containers and the text of Zoe's life intersected. Zoe made signs to act upon her world.

Negotiating. Zoe wrote four times during the year to do something that I had no word for, so I call it *negotiating.* Although she referred to it as "copying," I didn't agree with her so I label it differently. Zoe took a book from her bookshelf and seemed to be copying the words. As she copied, she changed some things that were written in the book. She substituted upper case for lower case letters and lower case letters for upper case letters. She moved to the next line on her paper when she ran out of room, not when the line changed in the book. Zoe was doing a lot of thinking and decision making as she wrote; she was not merely copying, because her writing was reflecting her understanding of concepts such as the one-to-one correspondence between upper and lower case letters, flexible use of line changing, and self-selection of books as resources.

Journal Writing. Zoe wrote journal entries three times during the year. She saw Sadie writing in her personal journal quite a bit and Zoe wanted to be like her big sister. Twice, early in the year, Zoe wrote in an old diary that Sadie gave to her. Once, she used a spiral-bound notebook. One of the early entries occurred after a disagreement with her mom (Fig. 3.14). Zoe retreated to her room and, once again using the Eastman (1960) book, *Are You My Mother?,* she copied part of the book. She copied 'mother,' 'my,' and 'snort' from the page in which a steam engine makes

FIG. 3.14. *Journal entry:* Snort is my mother.

a loud snorting sound. The text has *snort* in large red letters. The message, "Snort is my mother," reflects some of the anger Zoe was feeling at the time.

Later in the year, the day after Mother's Day, she wrote another journal entry. We had driven to the Mexican border and walked into Mexico for the day. It was well over 90°F when we returned to our car to drive home. Our car broke down halfway between the border and Tucson. We waited hours for a tow truck to finally rescue us. Later that day, Zoe wrote, "Today we had to wait two hours" (Fig. 3.15). She illustrated the page on which her writing appears and two more pages, as well.

I find it so interesting that when she wrote the earlier entry her spelling was quite conventional, but for the later one she seemed to not care as much about spelling

FIG. 3.15.   *Journal entry:* Today we had to wait two hours.

conventionally. Why is this? Perhaps she felt comfortable enough with her knowledge of written language to write her entry regardless of certain conventions. Perhaps she understood that in a private place, such as a journal, spelling mattered little because, in this case, the writer and her father were the only persons to read it. I chose not to ask Zoe about her invented spelling for fear that she might think I was overly concerned with conventional spelling and begin to limit her writing to words she could spell correctly. Lynn Rhodes (1981) discussed this in telling the story of a child who only wrote "I had a cat" for a story. The child did not ever own a cat, but wanted to write a story she could spell correctly.

Making Labels.   Zoe labeled things three times during the year. She made labels for her stuffed animals and she labeled the clay she manufactured and was selling at a sidewalk stand in front of our house (Fig. 3.16).

She understands that labels are short; they are compact for easy reading by a possible customer. This was nothing that she was taught directly; it is part of living in a society that uses labels. Her uses of written language at home reflect the written language community in which she lives.

Other Uses of Written Language.   Zoe wrote in a variety of other ways at home. She worked with Sadie on a newspaper, made envelopes for cards, wrote the alphabet for fun, dictated a story to me, wrote a poem, made a poster, made a record of Bo's growth resembling a record sheet from school, and wrote a sentence for reasons unknown. During our regular 'literacy patrols,' Zoe and I cleaned her room and looked for writing. We found notes, her journal, labels, and other items. We also found three things that were letter strings (Gentry, 1987), but neither of us knew what they were meant to say. Zoe wrote a total of 60 times at home during the year. The frequency and types of writing are summarized in Table 3.1.

I encourage you to develop tables and categories for your research stories. Perhaps you could even draw a diagram to explain why or how certain things

FIG. 3.16.   *Label:* Play dough, by Zoe.

Table 3.1
Types and Frequency of Writing Zoe Completed at Home During Kindergarten

Type of Writing	Frequency
Notes–letters	15
Stories	7
Lists	6
Signs	6
Negotiating	4
Journal entries	3
Labels	3
Newspapers	2
Cards	2
Envelopes	2
Alphabet	2
Dictation	1
Poetry	1
Poster	1
Record	1
Sentence	1
Unknown	3
Total	60

happen in whatever it is you are studying. Diagramming, drawing sketches, making pictures, designing tables, and using other ways to present your findings enhance your understanding of what you know. When I look at Table 3.1 and see how many more notes Zoe has written than other forms of writing, many new and intriguing research questions enter my mind. Why notes? Is it like that for other kids? Why don't we have kids write more notes in school? Are notes useful for teaching kids things about written language? Why do we focus so much on writing stories in schools? Should we be thinking about other writing possibilities? What might those be? How can we find out what other functions of writing kids know and use? Organizing a story by categories and tables may help raise more questions as much as they help to increase our understanding of our primary question or focus.

A story that goes on for many years requires much gathering of information, writing of anecdotes, and collecting of samples or *artifacts*. I like using this term because it makes this work feel like an archeological dig; we search for important pieces of what it is that puzzles us. Sometimes an important piece may be a whole activity that can be contained in a span of time. Zoe's oral language during the writing of a newspaper is one such event. I describe it here and then, later in this chapter, compare it to an oral event in school.

Oral Language During Newspaper Writing

Zoe wrote two newspapers during the year. One afternoon, Sadie and Zoe decided to make one together, working on the kitchen table and overflowing onto the living room floor, sipping apple juice, which they referred to as coffee. They worked for well over 1 hour. They encouraged each other and offered verbal feedback as they progressed. I include parts of the transcription of the audiotape I made during their work together. The conversation during the putting together of the newspaper compares in interesting ways to the discussions at the writing center in school that I present later.

This conversation reflects intense immersion in the project. The talk supports the work by clarifying, complimenting, providing information, making suggestions, giving feedback, establishing direction, and helping the children remain compatible.

During the construction of the newspaper, Zoe made a picture; she asked Sadie to help with the spelling of a word. Zoe realized, after writing the word, that she had put the word upside down in relation to the picture. Here is a piece of the conversation:

Zoe: Oh no. I put it upside down. See the bird is upside down.
Sadie: That's Okay.
Sadie: Just turn the picture upside down.
Zoe: Then the word will be upside down.
Sadie: That doesn't matter. It can be a backwards bird. I heard of one of them before. They're crazy; they drive me nuts. They're fun.
Zoe: Eeeeeee, nah. I don't wanna drive you nuts.
Sadie: That didn't drive me nuts. It's fun.
Zoe: It's fun driving you nuts?
Sadie: Ummhmm [meaning yes].

The girls developed a support system for each other and for the task itself. They only talked about newspaper items, except when discussing the bowling party they had attended earlier in the day. It was the first time either of them had bowled.

Note, as the girls talk to each other, how they learn from each other and how Sadie, the older one, is surprised at Zoe's seriousness about dotting the letter *i*.

Zoe: How do I do an *i*? [Zoe is actually requesting a lower case *i*, but does not call it that. Sadie intuits that Zoe wants specific information.]
Sadie: It's a stick. [Sadie is working on her own item for the newspaper while the discussion about spelling is going on.]
Zoe: Just a plain stick?
Sadie: Yeah with a dot on top [looking over to check out Zoe's *i*].
Zoe: P ... i ... dot ... d ...
Sadie: [to mother] Oh, she really did put a dot on the *i*.

This mutual help and support and feedback made the production of the newspaper truly cooperative in nature. Zoe was quite pleased to be part of the newspaper production. She responded positively to suggestions from her sister in an editorial relationship.

The children determined what materials they would need as the project progressed. They gathered the correct size paper, the stapler and staples, cardboard, crayons, markers, and pens. As they progressed through the activity, they reported their progress to each other. Sadie said that she had finished seven pages; Zoe had done two. One of Zoe's pages is the story of a disagreement between two individuals (Fig. 3.17).

The importance of the job of putting together a newspaper led the children to discuss certain aspects of the paper. Sadie was designing the front page; Zoe thought it was an advertisement for the newspaper.

Zoe: Sadie, we'll make that be a sign, okay?
Sadie: I want this to be the front page.
Zoe: No ummm. That's the sign to umm …
Sadie: What do you mean that's the sign? Zoey, this is gonna be the newspaper.
Zoe: That's the first page.
Sadie: Okay.

Later on in the production, Zoe was working with a piece of cardboard:

FIG. 3.17.   *Article in a newspaper.*

Zoe: Sadie, put cardboard under this and it could be the cover of the book.
Sadie: I already made the cover.
Zoe: Of the book?
Sadie: We're not doing a book. We're doing a newspaper.
Zoe: We can do a book, too. Sadie, should this be a hardcover book?
Sadie: I don't know. Let's just think about the newspaper while we're doing the newspaper.
Zoe: Okay ... What are we doing, again, after this?
Sadie: Get off it, Zoe.
Zoe: Sadie, wait. Make it a book. Staple the whole thing.
Sadie: No, 'cause this is how real newspapers are.
Zoe: Nooo. I don't want it like that.
Sadie: Okay. [This newspaper will be stapled.]

The piece remained a newspaper and was auctioned off. Zoe wanted it to go for $88, but was happy to get her half of $.22, the highest bid at the kitchen table.

The work of Halliday (1977, 1988) influenced my understanding of oral language more than anyone else's I read. As mentioned in chapter 2, Halliday discussed registers as the use and type of oral language specific to a setting and the relationships among the individuals there. We use many different registers when we speak. When we are at home with our families, we talk in a certain way—that is a register. When we are in the classroom with children, our language use is different; it is a different register.

I offer one further example to explain registers. Our conversation with our medical doctor is typically quite different from our conversations with our friends when we paint a room together. Halliday's work explains why there is a difference. The differences in registers of oral language occur because of the type of relationships we have with people (he called this *tenor of relationship*). Another part of the difference in registers has to do with the setting we are in and the subject matter we are dealing with. While painting a room, we might talk about the room, the color, and other parts of the job. Once we are busy painting, the conversation usually drifts to other things such as vacations we want to take, music, sports, sex, and more. The language used during the painting of a room can be broad because of the nature of our relationship with our copainters and the fact that we don't need to constantly discuss the job as we work at it.

The language used when visiting a medical doctor is quite different, as we focus on our bodies. The discussion is limited to medicine with few diversions. This is because of the nature of our relationship with our doctor and the subject (our physical condition). Talk with a doctor is a more specific register than talk with copainters who are friends. We can tell a lot about an activity by listening to the register of oral language.

Sadie and Zoe used a unique register when they worked on the newspaper. They were dealing with the subject matter of newspaper production. The register is complex because it is based on their relationship, what they are working on, and their writing activity. Their interest in the process of newspaper production rivets their oral language to that activity. I return to the use of registers to make sense of writing and oral language in school.

What a rich and varied writer's life Zoe was leading at home! She played many roles: author of notes, letters, and stories, list writer, sign maker, negotiator, journal writer, label designer, and more. Now, let's look at Zoe's life as a writer in school.

Zoe's Writing at School

I am now at a point in this story that is somewhat scary to me. The fear comes from a tension that rests in the differences I found between home and school writing. The differences were surprising and the tension they nurtured forced my relationship with Ms. K, Zoe's kindergarten teacher, to be tenuous at best. The fear, quite frankly, is of being labeled a 'teacher basher,' which is not what I intend to do in this section. Rather, I want to show the differences between home and school and raise some questions.

Zoe referred to the writing that she did at school as "work". She said, "It is writing center work", when I asked her about it. Since Ms. K made virtually all the decisions about what children would write in school, Ms. K established the categories of writing that I use in the sections that follow. The teacher did this by telling the children what each type of work was called: "This is your spelling list," or, "Today you will make a book at the writing center."

One facet of framing our stories in the literature is that we often find other writers supporting what we want to say. Sometimes they say it more poignantly. Carol Edelsky and Karen Smith (1984) summarized some writers' school lives in a way that fit Zoe's kindergarten experience:

> Putting pen to paper in school is usually an activity where a child writes out someone else's intentions, where prerequisite pragmatic conditions (like having a less informed audience when writing for the purpose of informing) are not met. In school writing, … one or more systems of written language are often missing altogether (as in workbook exercises) or the connections between the pragmatic system and the other three [semantics, syntax, and graphophonics] are distorted or severed. When either of these conditions obtain, what is engaged in and produced is not an instance of genuine writing because … essential features are missing. (p. 24)

It is not a pleasant quote, yet it is one that I showed my wife, friends, and colleagues once I found it because I felt relieved and reaffirmed. I felt this way because I had found other writers and researchers writing about the sensitive topic of writing in school as not being all that it could.

When Zoe started kindergarten, I decided to keep track of her written language development even more systematically than I had in the past. I had returned to graduate school full time and I arranged my schedule so that I could be a parent volunteer in her classroom 1 day each week. I also kept careful track of her writing at home.

Keeping track of a student systematically changes the student. Zoe began to keep track of her own writing because I was keeping track of it. She was essentially a coresearcher in this project. At first, I was concerned about this. Perhaps I wouldn't learn about the typical young writer if Zoe was a coresearcher. I decided that rather than study Zoe's writing from a distance, I wanted her to be active in the research. With her as a coresearcher, I could learn about the many possibilities of written language with someone who was willing to explore those possibilities—Zoe.

Zoe's kindergarten teacher, Ms. K, allowed me in her classroom as a helper. Occasionally, she let me teach songs to the children or read them a book, but most of the time she wanted a second adult in the room to help manage the many activities she planned. The room was set up with many centers: housekeeping, blocks, painting, clay, and more. There were five centers that were set up at tables: listening, art, math–science, writing, and reading. Ms. K was always at the reading center during the first 30 minutes of center time. Here the children worked with her on activities from the district's basal reader.

The five centers set up at tables were the required centers. The children had to finish an activity at their required center before they could choose to play at one of the many other centers around the room. There were five required centers because there are 5 days in a typical school week. Zoe, for example, would be at one center on Monday, a different one on Tuesday and so on, covering each required center once each week. This meant that Zoe was required to write in school once each week. There was a nonrequired printing center that had a typewriter, some old worksheets, and rubber stamps of the alphabet; Zoe rarely elected to go there.

Ms. K was a heroine for putting up with me. She knew I was a graduate student and she knew that I had more than 16 years of teaching experience and there I was—a parent volunteer in her classroom. She had to feel some degree of discomfort. Once, I suggested that the basal might not be the best way to teach beginning reading and that perhaps children might enjoy visiting the writing center more than once each week. Ms. K said she liked to do things the way she always had. She knew some people were getting into whole language, but she did not choose to do so. She said, "I know what you're trying to do here." She feared I was there to take over, to change her.

Ms. K was angry and threatened. I backed off. I didn't want to be disinvited from the class. I didn't want to have my daughter's teacher feel angry at me. I told her I understood that she did not want to change and that I appreciated the pressure she felt when I was in the classroom. I said that I would be as unobtrusive as I could. I truly did want to watch and learn. I knew that Sadie had very traditional teachers in her kindergarten and first-grade experiences, and she had become an avid reader and writer. I wanted to learn how Zoe developed as a writer, so I needed to observe and learn from what unfolded during the school year.

In the following pages, I describe Zoe's written language activity at school. As a side trip consistent with the one I took with the evidence I collected at home, I present and analyze some of the oral language that took place around her writing activity.

Books.   The most common activity at the writing center was the making of books. Zoe had to copy the teacher's model to make a book that looked just like that model. *The Farm Book,* for example, contained pictures of things that began with *F.* Zoe colored teacher-provided pictures and put them in the book in the order that matched the model. Figure 3.18 shows a page from the *Love is ... book.* Zoe drew a picture of me and copied the word *dad* from the teacher's list of things children could include in the book.

Copying Letters and Words.   Another common activity at the writing center was copying letters. Figure 3.19 shows one example of the 13 times during the year that Zoe copied letters only. Sometimes the teacher had the children copy rows of letters and leave a line at the bottom of the page to copy a word two or three times on that final line of the paper. Zoe completed 11 sheets with rows of letters and a word. I call this copying because the letters and words had to be rendered exactly as the teacher's model. There was no room for negotiating.

Initial Consonants, Individual Words, and Missing Letters.   The type of initial consonant sheet that Zoe did eight times during the year is shown in Fig. 3.20. Other worksheets (Fig. 3.21) required that she copy a single word at a time. Five times during the year, Zoe had worksheets that required that she fill in missing letters in a sequence (*A B C __ E F*).

FIG. 3.18. *Page of "Love is ..." book.*

FIG. 3.19. *Copying letters.*

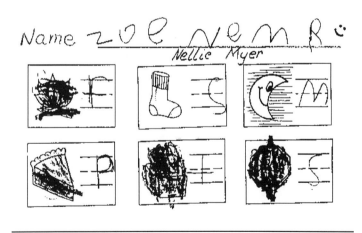

FIG. 3.20. *Initial consonant sheet.*

Spelling. During the final weeks of the school year, Zoe had spelling lists in kindergarten. She never had a spelling test, but the children worked with the spelling words when they were at the reading center with Ms. K and again at the writing center where they might write the spelling words two or three times. Figure 3.22 shows one of the spelling lists. Zoe put eyes in the word *look* because some of the

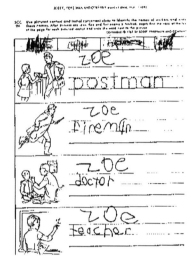

FIG. 3.21. *Copying letters.*

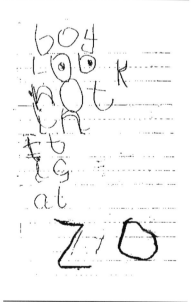

FIG. 3.22. *Spelling list.*

other children were doing that. They laughed quite a bit about this and Ms. K laughed, too.

Record Sheets.   Three times during the year, the children filled out record sheets. Record sheets involved the children in looking at something and writing about it. One day the children looked at a picture of a ladybug. They filled out the record sheet shown in Fig. 3.23. Record sheets were the only time that Zoe was allowed to use invented spelling during a teacher-required writing activity.

Other Types of Written Language.   The remaining kindergarten writing experiences occurred infrequently in the classroom. Zoe did each of these activities once: wrote the days of the week to make a calendar; wrote "Peter Rabbit" multiple times; wrote "Run, run as fast as you can. You can't catch me I'm the Gingerbread Boy"; traced around a word; and wrote the entire alphabet (upper case).

Table 3.2 summarizes the types of written language activity in which Zoe engaged during her school days in kindergarten. She was required to write a total of 78 times during the year. Most of the writing involved copying from the teacher's model.

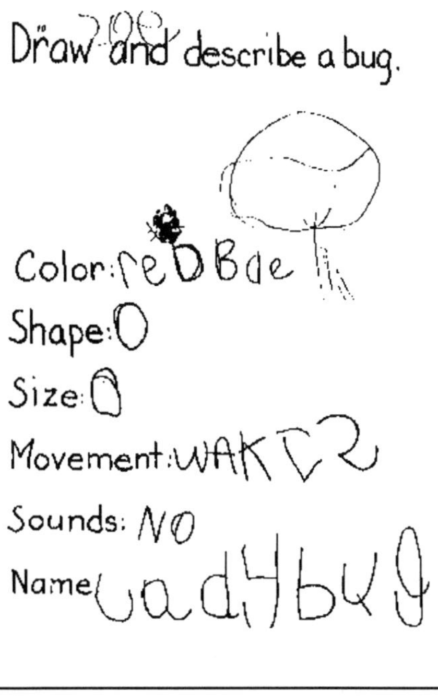

FIG. 3.23.   *Ladybug record sheet.*

TABLE 3.2
Types and Frequency of Writing Completed at School in Kindergarten

Type of Writing	Total
Books	22
Rows of same upper–lower case letter	13
Rows of letters and one word	11
Initial consonants	8
Individual words	7
Missing alphabet letters	5
Spelling word lists	4
Record sheets	3
Calendar	1
Phrase: Peter Rabbit	1
Refrain: Gingerbread Boy	1
Configuration	1
Alphabet: Upper case	1
TOTAL	78

When I began to collect and study Zoe's written language activity in school, I spent many days sitting at the writing center. She was always at the center with the same five children; they were the members of her committee and traveled to all the required centers together each week of the school year. I helped children cut things, clean up, fit clips into holes to bind their books, refill empty staplers, and so on. Eventually, the children got used to my presence and would pretty much go about their writing business, paying little attention to me. An indicator of their lack of interest or inhibition during my presence was their oral language. Once they were comfortable with, and stopped directing all conversation toward me, they enjoyed each others' company. I became intrigued with their discussions as they worked.

I spent a few months carefully writing down as much of what they said as I could. Some days I taped the discussions in order to listen to them over and over. I wrote down the topics of their discussions to see if there were any patterns to their conversations during their writing time. When they were working on the required writing activity, the children talked about various things that had to do with their assignment. They often talked about what color they would use. If an assignment had a required number of things to write or items to glue on, they discussed the number of items left to reach completion. Occasionally, pieces or pages of a book would get misplaced and they would discuss and search for the lost pieces. The children also talked about who would clean up what.

The members of this committee knew they were in school and doing work. Some days they talked about work. They would assert that what they were doing was, indeed, work. They talked about it being hard or easy work. They also evaluated each others' work. They knew that Ms. K liked neat work and neatness was a criteria they applied to each others' work during these discussions. This all seems like conversation that one would expect at a writing center. What intrigued me is that discussions about their writing and their work were not typical at the center.

Typical discussions at the writing center were not about writing at all. As the children cut, copied, or pasted, they discussed which center they would go to when they completed the required center. Some days they would all talk like babies; "me no have a bwu [blue] cwayon [crayon]." They acknowledged this as baby talk and prolonged these discussions until they became loud and Ms. K would remind them to work quietly. The children talked about their bicycles because one of them rode her bike to school. They discussed jewelry when one of them was wearing some. One of the girl's mothers is a cosmetologist so discussions sometimes went in the direction of hairstyles. The children talked about their families and what different family members did for a living. They talked about holidays and their fears (around Halloween). On some days, the children at the center would whisper a song and all would sing as they worked. As individual birthdays approached, they would discuss their ages.

When Ms. K would remind them to be quiet, the conversation would cease for a few minutes. When they began to talk, they would remind each other to be quiet. The issue of friendship was a common topic as the members of the committee reaffirmed their friendships. They talked about Ninja turtles and other cartoon or movie characters. Near the end of center time, snack was an inevitable topic of conversation as they became hungry.

When I write a longer story, I think about the different categories of things that appear in what I collect. I sometimes write ideas on index cards to look for patterns and ways to organize them. Figure 3.24 discussions during work at a center is a chart that organizes discussions at the writing center. I realized that the children

FIG. 3.24. *Topics of discussion during work on required writing activites.*

either talked about the task (their writing), or they discussed issues not related to the task. I organized the chart by those categories. Then I put each type of discussion in its place and studied the chart.

Eventually, the children's discussions began to make sense to me in light of my own past. My father worked in a factory his whole life. Some Saturdays he would need to go to work because they had a big order to fill. The factory assembled things. Sometimes they glued brand names on items; other times they might have a contract to assemble shower curtain sets. The possibilities were endless. On a rare Saturday, he would allow me to go to work with him. This meant that the work was not physically demanding and that we would be finished by noon.

My father found me a place on the assembly line, although it was usually more of a circle than a line on weekends because there were fewer employees working on Saturdays than during the week. We worked at whatever the job was, attempting to complete as many as possible. The discussions of my fellow workers fascinated me as the child-among-adults. They talked about baseball, sex, the weather, and many other things, sometimes in English, some times in Spanish, and sometimes in Haitian Creole. (The one thing that they rarely discussed was their work.)

They didn't talk about applying the glue or sealing a box. They never mentioned when they needed a tool or were reaching for a particular piece. Their discussions could focus on a broad variety of other subjects because they knew the process of the work so well that discussing it would seem bizarre. Picture yourself peeling potatoes for potato salad. If you were working with others as you peeled and cut potatoes, think how strange they would consider you if you said, "Oh, wow, I'm going to choose that potato. Here I go. Oh, I've got it. Now, I'm starting to peel it. I'm peeling it with the peeler going away from me. Now I see an eye. Oh my, I better cut that out right away!" Such conversation is not necessary because of the repetitive nature of the work.

The same was true of factory work. Occasionally I would need help and someone would laugh as someone else helped me. But the overall procedure was that we worked and talked about things not related to our work. So it was with the kindergarten writing center.

For the most part, the oral language at the center was similar to the oral language of factory work. The two have very similar registers. The workers did their writing, for example writing *h* after *h* after *h*, line after line after line. As they did so, they discussed the many topics listed earlier.

What did I learn from this? First, that my life, my own past, helps me understand the nature of something that happens in the classroom. My lived experiences frame each experience and my understanding of that experience. Second, that there is a relationship between written language and oral language. Discussions during writing can provide a window into the nature of the activity. By paying attention to the register, I can learn a lot about the writers' view of their written language activity. I can get a sense of whether or not they are invested in the work as something mundane and droll or as something intense, exciting, and mentally demanding. Conversations that center around things far from the task (hairstyles and bicycles) might indicate less of a meaning-making process and more of a factory work orientation.

Earlier, I discussed the register of oral language during newspaper production. Zoe's oral language during that activity focused on the use of writing as a way of making meaning (Wells, 1986). Oral language during school writing, with a factory register, reflected Zoe's relationship with the teacher and with her peers and did not focus as much on the making of meaning with written language. The teacher's power in the classroom is clear: She provided the activity, decided on criteria for success, and demanded certain behavior during writing time. The children were laborers, much like the factory workers I described.

The side trip into oral language taught me to listen to children as they work or play because their conversations reveal much about their investment and learning in that work or play. Discussions about their activity (including questions, problems, thoughts, discoveries, and collaboration) demonstrate their commitment, motivation and passion, and provide insights into what they are learning.

A Surprise: A Writer's Underground

An exciting discovery I made one day in the kindergarten classroom almost escaped my attention. Zoe took a small piece of paper from the print center and quickly wrote her name and phone number on it. She gave it to her friend, whose name begins with an *R* and said, "Now give me your phone number." R said her number as Zoe wrote.

"Put my name on it so you know it's my number," her friend said.

"Oh, your name is too long to write," Zoe answered. "I'll just put an R and know that it's you."

In a matter of seconds, the girls had each other's phone number and play resumed as usual at the center. It was an exciting moment because the children had used written language for an important purpose. They had exchanged phone numbers, enabling further communication after school (Fig. 3.25). Ruth Hubbard (1989)

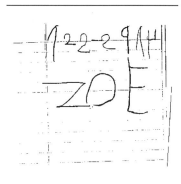

FIG. 3.25   *Evidence of the underground:* a phone number.

referred to this type of writing as part of the "underground, the unofficial literacy" (p. 291) of the classroom because it typically occurs outside of the curriculum without teacher knowledge.

Another instance of underground writing was when Zoe found a form for writing a friendly letter at the print center. She had rummaged through a pile of old worksheets that Ms. K placed at the center for the children to play with. Zoe wrote a note to her mom (Fig. 3.26): "Mom, Two chickens hatched. Your kid, Zoe Meyer (kiss, hug, kiss)," reporting the hatching of incubated eggs in the classroom.

The story of Zoe's life as a writer across the two settings of home and school is a powerful story for me because of who she is—my daughter. I attempted to be thorough in the telling and to give you a sense of the differences in the nature of her writing and some oral language, too. Now, I attempt something that I encourage you to do. I am going to pose a theory based on the story I told. I encourage you to be theoretical about your stories; make tentative decisions about why things happened as they did, and 'try on' a theory to see if it explains things in the present story and in future stories.

FIG. 3.26. Mom, Two chickens hatched. Your kid, Zoe Meyer (kiss, hug, kiss).

A THEORY

My theory, based in the story of Zoe's writing during the year of her life when she was in kindergarten, is rather simple: Writers have agendas. When a writer sets out to write something, he or she has a purpose for his or her writing. A writer's agenda comes from the writer's lived experiences as they unfold within a given setting and even across settings. He or she writes because he or she wants to know others are doing chores while he or she is doing chores, or a writer writes because he or she is part of a family and wants his or her needs on the grocery lists, or he or she writes because he or she wants to please a teacher or parent.

Writers' agendas are swayed and influenced by their situations. If they know they are going to the bakery, they might write a note asking if they can invite a friend. If curious about who is on the phone, they might pass a note to the person on the phone asking, "Who is it?" These are uses of writing that flow from the writer as he or she lives in a literate family and neighborhood. Someone in a powerful position can influence a writer's agenda. A father can say, "If you want something from the store, put it on the shopping list." A teacher can say, or imply, "If you want to succeed in this classroom, you will write the alphabet on this piece of paper."

The agenda is something personal that occurs in a social setting. A writer, by listening to who he or she is and the nature of the situation, makes decisions about his or her agenda. He or she might decide that he or she does not care enough for chocolate chips to put them on the shopping list. He or she can also decide not to complete the teacher's worksheets. The writer must make decisions based on the information at hand and an awareness of consequences. Not having chocolate chips may be acceptable; dealing with a dissatisfied teacher may not be acceptable to the writer. The writer decides what to put on or take off of his or her writing agenda.

Zoe learned a lot more when she could choose what to write about. At those times, she was following her own agenda. She let the teacher's items be part of her writing agenda because Zoe knew that survival in school rests on doing what a teacher demands. Zoe placed items on her agenda at home because she was interested in what she was writing. The idea of an agenda makes me wonder what would happen if a child could dictate his or her own agenda more, even in school. Much of the research on written language I presented previously supports this idea. Children learn more about language when they are allowed to explore language, raise their own questions about language, and come to some resolution (even if temporary) about their questions.

When left to her own devices, Zoe chose to involve herself in writing activities that were challenging and meaningful to her; they were also situations in which she was busy learning and using oral language to support her learning. When someone else imposed a writing agenda on her, Zoe's oral language rarely dealt with the writing activity and the activity itself assumed a 'produce and be done' mentality rather than an intense investment of time, ownership, and energy.

It is probably clear that I was not happy with Zoe's writing experiences at school. My passion and commitment to her and my motivation to learn more about writing have led to my life's work: understanding literate lives. I hope to continue to gain insights into writers' agendas—young writers' and not-so-young writers'.

REFLECTING ON THIS LONG STORY

I learned a lot about Zoe and written language as a result of the story I wrote. My writing helped me to organize and formalize my thinking and, eventually, led to this book being written. Our stories teach us. We change, our practice changes, our motivation and passion changes.

Other stories might affect other teachers when we share them in groups (see chap. 4) or by formal publication. Gordon Wells (1994) worked with nine teachers to write the stories of their classrooms. Each of the teachers chose an area of classroom activity that intrigued or troubled them or aroused their curiosity. They worked as a support group to nurture their research activity as they collected evidence, read some of the professional literature that dealt with their interest area, and wrote their stories.

My story about Zoe changed me and it changed Zoe. She talks about her writing with me and others who are willing to listen because she was a coresearcher in this project. Zoe is a literacy researcher who enjoys studying her growth over time. Her dad is a literacy researcher who keeps learning from her and other children, their teachers, and their parents. One story, of Zoe, leads to others' stories as I read to frame the original story and it leads to other questions. The process of questioning and looking renews itself and that process of renewal renews us as teachers; it keeps us fresh, excited, and curious.

A TEACHER'S STORY OF ONE STUDENT

A fine example of passionate questioning, commitment, and motivation to act follows, as Kara tells the story of Robert.

* * *

After teaching for 6 years, I was beginning to feel very secure in my teaching abilities. However, there are always areas in which I try to look for improvement. This area was the assessment of my students in the classroom. If all of my students had the same learning styles, same interests, and the same learning experiences, assessment would be simple. However, we all know that there is no such thing as that type of ideal classroom! That is why I was excited to be finishing up my last year of my master's degree with a two semester sequence on assessment. In my undergraduate classes I was not prepared at all for assessing students, especially on an individual basis.

I had heard horror stories about assessment classes. A colleague had taken one and said that all I would do was to sit for 3 hours each week and look at bell curves. As I left the first night's class, I knew this was going to be different because we spent the evening making up our syllabus as a class so that we would study things that we as educators could actually use in the classroom. Now there was a new twist. I was fortunate enough to have an instructor who not only allowed as to do a year-long study on anything we wanted to do dealing with assessment, but this class let me experience how important it is to read as many books and articles as I could get my hands on. Although I never considered myself an avid reader, my interest was triggered by articles and books that addressed the needs I was facing as a teacher, particularly the need to meet the needs of struggling readers and writers.

After reading many books on different subjects it was now time to try and pick a purpose for my year-long study. I realized that my purpose was to examine the extent to which a child's stress affects his or her literacy development. My motivation for researching this topic was that in today's society, educators are seeing more children who are forced to deal with tremendous amounts of stress. These obstacles include such things as home environment, how a child's socioeconomic status affects self-esteem, and how children deal with the stress of teacher's expectations, especially children from low socioeconomic situations. So many times, as teachers, we assess children on the basis of our class needs (whole groups tests that evaluate the class) rather than on individual needs. I decided to do my research on an individual child in order to increase my awareness and understanding of a single learner in my classroom. I wanted to look at a specific child as a window into issues of assessment in general and this child in particular—a child who was experiencing stress.

The next step was to pick a student in my classroom who fit this mold. That is where Robert came into the picture. Robert was a 10-year-old White male in my fourth-grade class. He was of low socioeconomic status. His family was considered nontraditional. Robert had been recently replaced into his home after being in foster care for 1½ years. His mother had recently returned from being in drug rehabilitation for 1 year. Robert's father had been in the state penitentiary for 4 years for stealing auto parts and abusing his wife of 11 years.

Besides being a victim of parents who abused drugs and alcohol, Robert had also been a victim of sexual abuse when he was 4 years old and has yet to receive any kind of counseling.

Students like Robert have so many obstacles to deal with that it is hard for them to succeed as students. The obstacles I focused on with Robert included low self-esteem, pressure from peers, unstable family life, low socioeconomic status, and inconsistent teacher expectations. All of these factors served to define stress in Robert's life.

Robert

Robert indeed lacked both self-esteem and motivation. He was not only rejected by his parents and teachers, but also by his peers. Robert expressed his feelings about himself in his journal (Fig. 3.27).

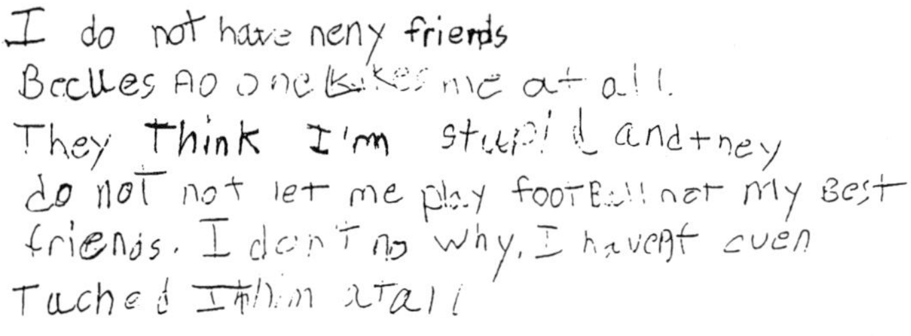

FIG. 3.27. *Journal entry*: I do not have any friends because no one likes me at all. They think I'm stupid and they do not let me play football, not my best friends. I don't know why. I haven't even touched them at all.

This was one of many pieces of writing in which I felt Robert was crying out for help. Robert also dealt with many teachers who had low expectations of him. Teachers simply would give up on Robert because he did not "fit" into their classroom. They would often roll their eyes when I mentioned Robert. I saw him isolated, in the hall, on many days during his year in third grade (the year before he entered my classroom).

A book I referred to many times during my study on Robert was *Lives on the Edge* by Valerie Polakow (1993). She cited Kenneth Clark as saying that disadvantaged youths':

> expendability begins in the early stages of their education where they are subjected to inferior schools and low standards of learning. Early in their lives they are programmed to be victims of the prophecy that they cannot benefit from the standards and quality which are provided for children from more privileged groups. This pattern of inferior education, of low standards and expectations, continues through secondary schools and culminates in failures, dropouts, and pushouts. (p. 148)

These expectations often lead students like Robert to failure and they often drop out or become behavior problems.

Over the course of the year, Robert and I developed a very positive relationship. I worked with his mom to help her find a job and talked him through the intensity of the return of his father into the home setting. I accepted his thoughts about life as legitimate and important, and I welcomed his rather silly sense of humor as an important part of our class. The other children knew he was 'different' (poor) and didn't treat him kindly at the beginning of the year. However, they saw that Robert was important to me so they gave him some positive attention. I became Robert's confidant, and he often wrote notes to me and began to share his feelings through his reading and writing (Fig. 3.28).

Robert needed to have learning experiences that would fit him personally, otherwise he was not interested. I learned that Robert, as a stressed student, was less willing than were nonstressed students to view learning as an adventure into unknown territory. He wanted things familiar. The first month of school, Robert seemed timid toward his writing abilities (Fig. 3.29). His stress seemed linked to his assessment of himself.

Dear Jornel,
I hope I have a
good week at my school.
I do not like my dad
when he drinks been
or wine, wissey.
My teacher is Mrs. Osborne
I like her alot because
she is pretty. And
like her because
she is nice.

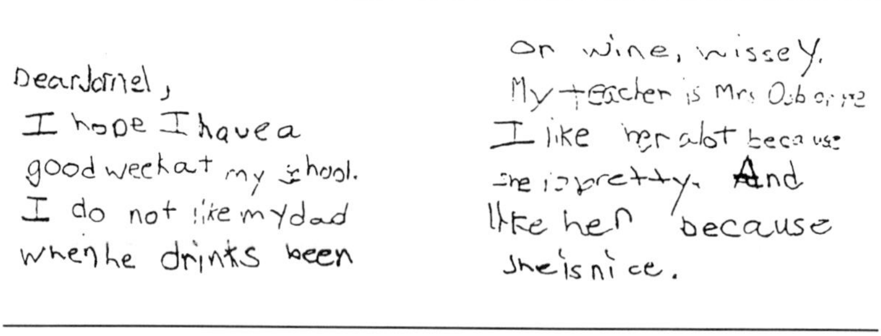

FIG. 3.28. *Journal entry:* Dear Journal, I hope I have a good week at my school. I do not like my dad when he drinks beer or wine, [or] whiskey. My teacher is Mrs. Osborne. I like her a lot because she is pretty. And I like her because she is nice.

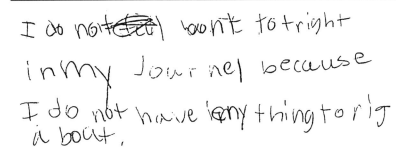

FIG. 3.29. *Journal entry:* I do not want to write in my journal because I do not have anything to write about.

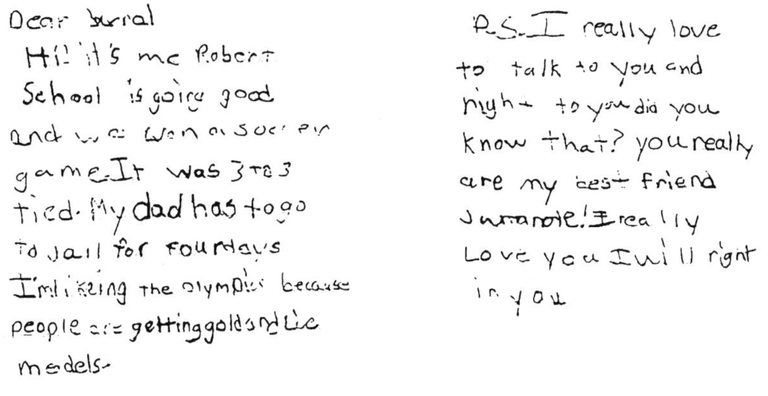

Dear Jurnal
Hi! it's me Robert
School is going good
and we won a soccer
game. It was 3 to 3
tied. My dad has to go
to jail for four days
I'm liking the olympics because
people are getting gold and silver
medels-

P.S. I really love
to talk to you and
right to you did you
know that? you really
are my best friend
Jurnole! I really
Love you I will right
in you

FIG. 3.30. *Journal entry:* Dear Journal, Hi, it's me Robert. School is going good and we won a soccer game. It was three to three, tied. My dad has to go to jail for four days. I'm liking the olympics because people are getting gold and silver medals. P.S. I really love to talk to you and write to you. Did you know that? You really are my best friend, Journal! I really love you. I will write in you.

He believed he couldn't write and didn't like to read or write. Perhaps this is because somewhere a teacher had low expectations of him. However, as time passed, Robert's attitude toward his writing improved, as evidenced by Fig. 3.30.

Throughout the school year, Robert's motivation to write blossomed. He became more willing to write when he was encouraged to make connections with his out-of-school experiences. I supported him in this process. For example, Robert wrote about Sam the octopus (Fig. 3.31). Sam wanted to be liked, but no one would ever invite him over to play or be his friend. At the end of the story, Sam rescues his friends and becomes a hero. Finally,

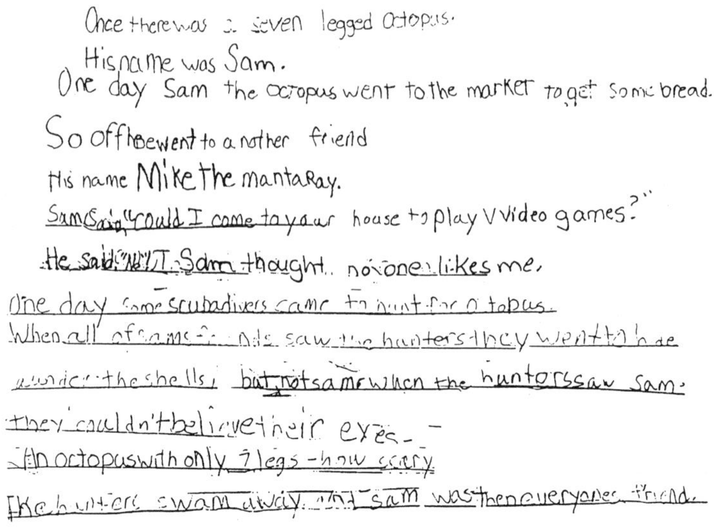

Once there was a seven legged Octopus.

His name was Sam.
One day Sam the octopus went to the market to get some bread.

So off he went to another friend

His name Mike the mantaRay.

Sam said "Could I come to your house to play Video games?"

He said "No!" Sam thought. no one likes me,

One day some scuba divers came to hunt for octopus.

When all of Sam's friends saw the hunters they went to hide

under the shells, but not same when the hunters saw Sam.

they couldn't believe their eyes. –

An octopus with only 7 legs – how scary

The hunters swam away and Sam was then everyones friend.

FIG. 3.31. *Story:* Once there was a seven-legged Octopus. His name was Sam. One day Sam the octopus went to the market to get some bread. So off he went to another friend. His name [was] Mike the manta ray. Sam said, "Could I come to your house to play video games?" He said, "No!" too. Sam thought, "No one likes me." One day some scuba divers came to hunt for octopus. When all of Sam's friends saw the hunters, they went to hide under shells, but not Sam. When the hunters saw Sam, they couldn't believe their eyes. An octopus with only seven legs ... how scary. The hunters swam away and Sam was then everyone's friend.

people like Sam. Not only was Robert writing about himself, he also put the same hat and shirt on Sam that he wore. Robert is Sam and Sam is Robert and both of them were welcomed in the classroom by me. My relationship with Robert was making school a place to express, grow, experiment, and—most importantly—be safe.

When our class studied pioneers, we kept diaries we would carry with us along the Oregon Trail. Robert liked to write in his diary because he would fantasize and write about life as he would like it to be. As we shared our diaries, Robert gained the admiration of some class members because he wrote expressive and interesting entries (Fig. 3.32).

I also began to see more progress in Robert as a writer when he began his own diary at home (Fig. 3.33). This was also another line of communication for him to use to share his feelings with me. It was a way in which he made a connection between living at home and school activities.

In spite of all the improvement I had seen in Robert's literacy development, there were times when his anxiety level would skyrocket (Fig. 3.34).

During these times the question I would continually deal with was, "How do we as educators try to assess these children's literacy development when so much of their development revolves around their own personal lives?"

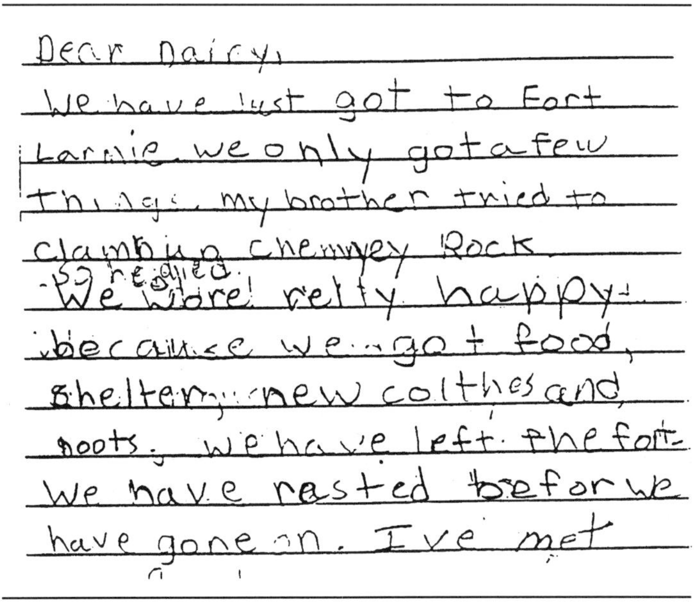

FIG. 3.32. *Pioneer Diary:* Dear Diary, We have just got to Fort Laramie. We only got a few things. My brother tried to climb up Chimney Rock. So he died. We were really happy because we got food, shelter, new clothes, and boots. We have left the Fort. We have rested before we have to go on. I've met new friends.

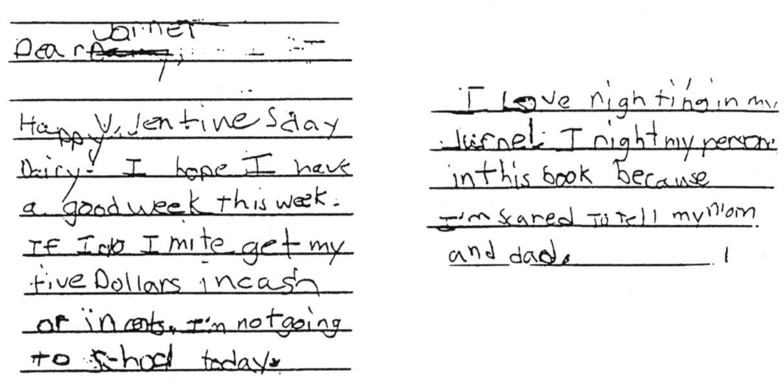

FIG. 3.33. *Journal entry:* Dear Journal, Happy Valentine's Day, Diary. I hope I have a good week this week. If I do I might get my five dollars in cash or cents. I'm not going to school today. I love writing in my journal. I write my person in this book because I'm scared to tell my mom and dad.

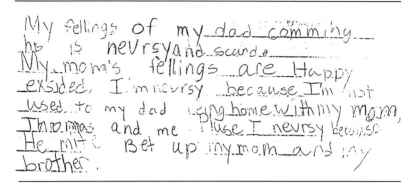

FIG. 3.34. *Journal entry:* My feelings of my dad coming home is
nervous and scared. My mom's feelings are happy [and] excited. I'm
nervous because I'm not used to my dad being home with my mom,
Thomas, and me. Plus I['m] nervous because he might beat up my
mom and my brother.

A View of Assessment

Although there is no one right answer, through all of my reading I came up with a solution
that has now satisfied my need to assess students like Robert. As teachers, we need to realize
that stress does affect our students' literacy development. It is our job to provide a safe
learning environment for our students. To do this, we need to become aware of the many
different strategies teachers can use to help them cope with stress. Once an educator
recognizes the coping styles a child is using, he or she can propose more effective strategies
to help the child cope with stress. There is no "quick fix." Teachers need to make available
resources to help guide children to combine strategies that will work best for them. I finally
learned through this study that I cannot eliminate a child's stress, because many of the
stressors are out of my control. I can only help to reduce some of the stress that may be
happening at school.

The best strategy I found with Robert was to discuss with him what his major stressor was
and try to work with him as a team to cope with it in the most effective manner. I worked
to understand who Robert was and to constantly help him explore choices for
actions—actions he could initiate for his own survival and growth. Educators can no longer
assess the classroom as a whole. Each child needs to be taken into consideration and be
assessed as an individual. This has made my teaching a more enormous job than it was prior
to the study. It also makes more urgent the need to make connections between children's
learning in school and personal–social development.

The present and future of children like Robert and their families demand a broad vision
and courageous leadership from educators of all levels, students, and parents. This will take
an extraordinary amount of dedication, care, and responsibility toward at-risk students.

This quote by Valerie Polakow (1993) summarizes my research with Robert:

> A classroom for a young child is a lifeworld; each year brings new forms of power, or
> possibility, of despair. As educators we are responsible for making school a place in which
> a child matters—a place away from the edges. (p. 162)

We educators need to realize that our role indeed has changed. I compare it to being somewhat like a detective—always searching for that missing part in a child's life.

This assessment project taught me two major things. First, the need to keep reading. It is so important to stay current and keep the blood flowing so that you always keep thinking about ways to improve yourself and your classroom. Second, to realize that we can not change a child's life, and there is no "quick fix." As educators, we need to provide coping strategies for these children and assess them on an individual basis, rather than the class as a whole.

I was glad I was able to get the chance to do a year-long study on something that interested me. I felt it was worthwhile, and would recommend the experience to any educator, especially newer teachers because I was able to have many questions answered that should have been answered long ago!

Thoughts on Framing

One of the hardest things for me to do as a writer in writing about Robert was to integrate my reading of other people's work into my own writing. So, quite honestly, I decided not to directly do that. On a first draft, I included quotes and cited many other people and wrote what some would consider to be quite a scholarly paper. But I didn't like it (even though I did use that paper as the culminating project for my master's degree). By weaving all those people in, I somehow lost my own voice. So, for the next few drafts, I just wrote. I thought a lot about what I had read and then wrote. That is how I am as a teacher. I think, read, teach, read, think, and so on. I am constantly integrating—taking possession of works (like Polakow's) that are important for me.

The piece on Robert in this chapter is based on some important reading. I include a list of things I've read at the end of this chapter so that readers will know whose thinking has helped me to frame my own thinking, analyzing, and writing.

* * *

REFLECTING ON THIS LONG STORY

As we read the story Kara wrote, it becomes clear that her passion, commitment, and motivation led her to read more, think more, be increasingly analytical of her classroom, and try a variety of strategies for assessing followed by action. In her story, she reveals something of her literate self (her increased interest in reading professional literature).

She is wrestling with the 'place' of the voices of others in her work. She uses many strategies and ideas from the books and articles she reads, but wants to take ownership of them to such a degree that they are dissolved into herself as a teacher. Therefore, she doesn't cite many works within the writing she does. I think her lack of citations throughout the text is partly because she is just beginning to do more professional reading. Many of the voices she used to frame her work were not kept separate because she had no reason to keep them separate except to show a master's project committee that she could write that "scholarly" way. When she rewrote Robert's story for this chapter, she decided to do it, as she says, "the way I wanted to write it, without worrying about who said what ... just saying what I wanted to say." Her present goal is not to continue scholarly writing with many citations; instead she engages in professional reading and then uses her writing to think on paper about her students.

For Kara, the integration of ideas and theories is more important than the person whose ideas or theories they are because she is going to put the ideas into practice rather than publications. Perhaps, if she continues to read, write, and think in a community of teachers that is also reading, writing, and thinking, the names of the individuals will become more important.

YOUR TURN: WRITE A LONG STORY

Now Kara and I, and other teacher-researchers, turn to you. It is time for you to write a longer story, time to focus in on what bothers you, intrigues you, motivates you, arouses your curiosity, or stirs your passion about the lives of children—not only to be a lifelong learner, but to be an advocate for children who need our voices so that theirs can be heard. Writing the stories of our teaching-learning lives is evidence of our commitment to the children we teach.

Does that seem like a challenge—almost a dare? It is. It is part of the challenge that is the emerging role of what it means to be a teacher; it means that you are an advocate and a researcher and a responsible professional. We take responsibility for studying our students, our classrooms, and our communities because those are the contexts in which we teach. It means we ask why and we ask how so that we can support change that supports our students' growth:

> Why and how students succeed or fail, we would argue, are inseparable questions whose answers must be found in the social manipulations that produce educational change. (Moll & Diaz, 1987, p. 311)

Vito Perrone (1991) asked:

> How do we express caring deeply about the students? About the society? How do we act out our citizenship, show our love for learning? Do we display an ongoing inquisitiveness about the world—how it works and why? Are we critical? Do we seek alternative explanations? Do we ask often about events being examined? What do they mean and why should it matter? Do we engage each other about such things? (p. 7)

Writing our stories, especially longer stories, helped us to answer some of the questions Perrone posed.

CLOSING NOTES ON THIS CHAPTER

You can see that long stories are a lot of work. They may cause us to focus on painful facets of teaching and learning, as well as help us celebrate our successes. They are a place for us to reflect, make decisions, make judgments and perhaps even theorize or generalize. This chapter gave two case studies of individual children as a powerful way to learn. You can also study a process, such as the implementation of portfolios in your classroom, or a small group of children working on a project over time, or a whole class. The possibilities are endless, but the most important parts are your passion about what you are studying, your commitment to the story, and your motivation to act as a reader, a writer (or oral storyteller), and a thinker.

SUGGESTED READING

Abrams, K., & Possell, L. E. (1993). Incorporating a brief social skills unit into the regular classroom setting. *School Psychology International, 14,* 149–158.

Brantlinger, E. (1992). Adolescents' interpretation of social class influences on schooling. *Journal of Classroom Interaction, 1,* 28.

Brookhart, S. M., & Rusnak, T. G. (1993). A pedagogy of enrichment, not poverty: Successful lessons of exemplary urban teachers. *Journal of Teacher Education,* 441.

Bullock, J. R., & Winter, J. (1992). Children without friends. *Childhood Education, 69,* 92–96.

Carini, P. F., (1982). *The school lives of seven children: A seven year study.* Grand Forks: North Dakota Study Group.

Dyson, A. H. (1993). *Social worlds of children learning to write in an urban primary school.* New York: Teachers College Press.

Elias, M. J. (1989). Schools as a source of stress to children: An analysis of casual and ameliorative influences. *Journal of School Psychology, 27,* 393–407.

Fox, L. C. (1989). Peer acceptance of learning disabled children in the regular classroom. *Exceptional Children, 56*(1), 50–59.

Garcia-Vazquez, E., & Ehly, S. W. (1992). Peer tutoring effects on students who are perceived as not socially accepted. *Psychology in the Schools, 29,* 500–512.

Greenwood, C. R., Carta, J. J., & Hall, V. R. (1988). The use of peer tutoring strategies in classroom management and educational instruction. *School Psychology Review, 17*(2), 81–94.

Lareau, A. (1989). *Home advantage.* London, England: Falmer Press.

Matheny, K. B., Aycock, D. W., & McCarthy, C. (1993). Stress in school-aged children and youth. *Educational Psychology Review, 5*(2), 16–37.

Polakow, V. (1993). *Lives on the edge: Single mothers and their children in the other America.* Chicago: The University Chicago Press.

Richardson, V., Casanova, U., Placier, P., & Guilfoyle, K. (1989). *School children at-risk.* New York: Falmer Press.

Taylor, D. (1991). *Learning denied.* Portsmouth, NH: Heinemann.

Voss, M. M., (1993). I just watched: Influences on one child's learning. *Language Arts, 70*(8).

chapter 4

Support Systems: Forums for Stories and Thinking

When I was a kid, this is what I thought:
Writers are strange beings born with "the gift."
They never stew over spelling.
They never forget the rules of punctuation.
They never worry whether or not to start a new paragraph.
They never have to rewrite in better cursive because of picky fifth-grade teachers.
They glide where I trudge.
They soar where I end up flat on my face.
For them writing is a piece of cake. Sitting alone in small attic rooms, they need only to stare out the gable window, and inspiration is sure to hit. Then they just write it all down, as simple as that! No help is needed.
These days I think something different: All of the above is pretty much garbage, especially the part about writers needing no help.

—Birdseye (1993, pp. 179–180)

In 1992, Tom Birdseye and I sat at his kitchen table, discussing *Just Call Me Stupid* (Birdseye, 1993), a book he had started about a boy who is suffering because he can't read. The child feels stupid; he's called stupid by the kids at school and by his father. Tom asked, "What would this kid feel like? And what could a teacher do to make him feel better about himself and help him become a good reader?" We sat and talked for a few hours and then Tom explained that he was getting a lot of help with this new book. He's talked to other people at the University of Arizona—teachers, kids, parents, and friends. He works as a writer by talking, thinking, daydreaming, and writing, and he prefers not to do this in isolation. His writing is based in social activity, his relationships with others, and his understanding of himself within those relationships. His creativity is a social act.

WRITING AS A SOCIAL ACT

How can writing be a social act? Don't most writers spend their days alone, writing? Who could possibly help me when my pencil is at the ready and my mind is focused and I'm about to enter a piece of paper? Is writing one of the loneliest things a person can do? Here I sit, alone in my cinderblock office with the door closed, writing—and writing that writing is a social act. I do spend many days with few other people close by. I might step out of the office on such days to chat with colleagues, but they seem to intuit that my visits are breaks from my work. They have learned to avoid interrupting me when my door is closed. In fact, our area of offices is often made up of closed doors. It's a sign to others that we're working … alone.

But I am rarely lonely or alone when I write. I am surrounded by loved ones. I love the books I have organized around me. I can see John Dewey over my right shoulder and Albert Einstein is on the wall above my monitor. I have audiotapes of music that I love. There are pictures of friends and family, and the wall behind me is covered with writing that children have sent to me over the past few years.

And you are here. I have to see you as I write or I can't write. Some days 'you' are my wife; other days you are a class of former students, or a teacher whose classroom I visited, or a colleague. In my mind, I have a relationship with you (some audience), and that means I am not alone. My audience is part of an important support group for my writing. To be quite honest, I like having you invisible. That way, I can imagine your responses to what I write. Writing is, in some ways, a very safe act. I avoid major risks when I write alone and read what I have written alone. As (and when) I feel braver, I allow people I know to be my audience.

There are substantive members of my support community. Sometimes my wife or daughters will read a section of a chapter in order to give me some feedback; or I might read it aloud to them for their opinions. Sometimes I read the piece aloud when no one but me can hear it because it's such a different piece when it's oral. One of the graduate students in our department is a very 'gentle reader.' Risa reads my work and asks questions that help me focus on what it is that I am trying to say. Colleagues read my work, too. Some of those colleagues live nearby, so I can drop off a piece in progress and ask for feedback. Others are far away and receive things via electronic mail or snail mail; I usually remember to include return postage and an envelope when sending things by snail mail. We also have a local TAWL (Teachers Applying Whole Language) group that serves as part of my support community. I also rely on groups of teachers with whom I do research as a source of mutual feedback, encouragement, and support. Most writers need a community of support to read our work and respond to it.

There are, then, many layers or types of community. There is the invisible reader of my work. There are the influences on my writing, most of whom have written books that surround me. There are real people that I know in my life. By far, the scariest of audiences is real people. When I read to others something I have written, I break into a sweat, my hands shake, and sometimes I can hear my heartbeat in my ears. This is not easy. I find myself instantly back in my childhood, seeking the approval of an audience and feeling very vulnerable to their criticism. There's a delicate balance here; I want to believe that I write for myself, as a way to learn, but I also write for a variety of audiences. Venturing out with my written work demands a safe community.

What does a community do?

Jane Hansen (1987) performed research in a classroom that was a community of writers and described writing communities this way:

> The members of the writing community rejoice in each other's accomplishments. We don't withhold information from each other because we fear someone else will do as well as we do. We share and others share with us. We want to learn, and through sharing we know what others know. This notion of everyone as a possessor of knowledge for everyone's use differs from previous systems, which insisted that every student keep to herself and which also established hierarchies of haves and have nots ... the community, a collective of diverse information, underlies the success of the writing. (p. 15)

I work to build a community like this for myself. It is a lot harder when we are not all committed to coming to the same classroom each day, but the work in developing the community is well-invested time. The community becomes a place where I can take risks and grow because of it.

My community consists of members of various groups in and outside of the university setting. You may find that there are other, more formal, groups of individuals who support each others' writing and the research that is often involved with such writing. In this chapter, I discuss some possible support systems for writers.

FINDING A SUPPORT SYSTEM

You may not have to build a support system from scratch. There are support systems already in place and these are discussed later. Finding a support system, or creating your own, is not always easy. It involves being honest with yourself about what you need from a group, working to clarify those needs, and understanding how you, as a unique individual writer, go about forming relationships. To make it even more complicated, this all keeps changing as you grow. The following sections are about honesty with yourself, relationships, and understanding and responding to what you need.

WHAT DO YOU NEED AS A WRITER?

I feel personal tension about support groups. It might sound as though I am contradicting myself, but there are times when I sincerely believe I could be a much better writer if I were all alone on a lush warm island with pencil, paper, the sun and surf, the sounds of the ocean, and lots of time for my mind to quiet down and focus. Although I know that my writing is something I do for me, it is also something I do in relationship with others. I need readers. To add further complexity, there are times when the thought of being alone with paper and pencil terrifies me. A writer wants to be alone, a writer needs to be alone, a writer doesn't want to be alone, a writer feels very much alone, a writer feels part of a group, a writer needs a group, a writer is alone, a writer isn't alone. So, which is it? It's all of these. The best I can do as I constantly and temporarily resolve these tensions (or use them to drive my writing), is to be honest about my needs at a given point in time and respectful of my commitment to others and myself. With that rather existential backdrop, I offer some thoughts on finding a group, making sure the group responds to your needs as a writer, and sustaining a support group.

Honesty

One of the best things a writer can do for him or herself is to be honest about what he or she needs by focusing on those needs and paying attention to intuitive 'nudges' that say that something is or is not working. We are coming to know what children require in order to discover and continue to construct their own literacy:

> The key is to set up an environment where there are many invitations to read and write, where reading and writing are juxtaposed and used for a variety of purposes, and where children have opportunities to meet and come to see themselves as authors. The environment should also be one where they see their teacher as an author and a learner. Each curricular component [should] provid[e] children with invitations to engage, see demonstrated, and come to value the strategies involved in authoring. Each curricular component [needs] a basis from which the authoring cycle can begin anew. (Harste & Short, with Burke, 1988, p. 168)

As adults, we need pretty much the same things. We need invitations to read and write, to write for a variety of purposes, and the opportunity to see ourselves as authors. We need colearners on our journey as writers and demonstrations of writing that we can emulate, discuss, depart from, and argue over. And, each writing experience needs to be viewed as the doorway into subsequent writing experiences for a lifetime of writing, thinking, reading, and learning.

Relationships

The nature of our relationships with the members of our support group is an integral part of the group's "life." Together, we create a construction zone (Newman, Griffin, & Cole, 1989) in which our writing takes place, is presented, and may be critiqued. We work as a group, within that zone, to create ourselves as thinkers, searchers, "re-searchers," readers, and writers. Choose this group carefully, with as much understanding of your needs and theirs as possible, so that you can see if your needs and expectations are mutual or (at least) mutually supportive.

Carolyn Heilbrun (1988) explained why writing our stories is hard work:

> What matters is that lives do not serve as models; only stories do that. And it is a hard thing to make up stories to live by. We can only retell and live by the stories we have read or heard. We live our lives through texts. They may be read, or chanted, or experienced electronically, or come to us, like the murmurings of our mothers, telling us what conventions demand. Whatever their form or medium, these stories have formed us all; they are what we must use to make new fictions, new narratives. (p. 37)

Our 'new fictions' (our stories) are nested in our relationships with others. Writing these stories, presenting them to ourselves and others, and living in and with the responses to our stories is the very stuff of being a writer. Staying centered as a writer means being honest and forming relationships. It also means that you get in touch with what you need.

What Do You Need From a Group?

Each of us, as writers, has different needs. You need to identify these needs so that you can make them public to the group. I call this *identifying and developing a desirable group process.* What do you envision the work of the group to be like? Do you want folks to spend time writing together in the same room, or would you prefer they arrive with things written and copies for all? Or do folks want things read aloud? Or would you like people on the meeting's agenda to send to you what is to be discussed so that you have time to read and reread the piece before meeting? Answering these questions will help you understand what you expect from a group. The way the group spends its time together is the group's process. You need to work together to create a group whose process is healthful for each member. Find a group willing to make the commitment to spend time together and to devote some of that time to identifying how members can have their needs accommodated.

One of my colleagues was in a group of writers who met regularly as each one worked on writing his or her thesis or dissertation. One of the most important things they did at their regular meetings was to give each person 5 minutes to "moan and groan," to complain about things that were getting in the way of their writing, things that weren't working well, and even things at their school that were bothering them.

Members who didn't need this time, didn't use it. Then, members were given 20 minutes each to focus on their writing. The focus time could be more intense because participants had ventilated some of their discomfort. They were able to move beyond issues requiring ventilation and could work on dealing with difficult areas in their writing, or celebrate successes or joys, or deal with other issues of the written piece and the writing process. The members of this group allowed each other to think aloud and to respond to each other's thinking; the focus person was allowed to say, "Let me finish this thought," or, "I want to think this out loud," or, "Tell me what you think for about 2 minutes." This way, the focus person controls the use of his or her focus time in the group.

If you are new as a group, and no members have previously been part of a writers' support group, you need to be willing to experiment together. Try different ways of spending your time together and save time at the end of each session for some sincere and honest evaluation of the way time was used (i.e., evaluate the group's process). Time is so precious to teachers and preservice teachers that we need to be honest with each other so that our time feels well-invested.

What Does a Group Need From You?

A writers' support group needs your time, your responsibility, your commitment, your motivation, and your passion. The group needs to know that you are a safe person with whom to interact, read, and share. They need to know that you can be counted on; thus, your involvement is a commitment and a responsibility that should not be taken lightly. You cannot schedule orthodontist appointments, aerobics, and other activities in this time slot. So, be reasonable and honest about what you can offer the group. Let them know, as early as possible, what you are willing to give and, as a group, work together to keep track of your commitment, especially if you sense it changing over time.

The group needs glue; it needs a cohesiveness that will sustain it through the times that come after that beginning honeymoon period when everyone is being so very nice, polite, and holding back quite a bit. You are checking each other out to see if this is the group for you. Again, as the group's life unfolds, it is important to see who seems to hold the group together and to acknowledge that person. The glue person is the one who makes sure that your next meeting time and place are planned before leaving the present meeting. He or she is the person who mails things to group members, reminds them of meetings, offers his or her home as a site for meetings, or has a 15-year-old who will do child care while you meet. Any or all of these characteristics contribute to the sustenance of the group.

I remember individuals like this in high school. They were the ones who were the most willing to have a party at their house; they also pushed the student council or class governing body to sponsor a dance or a memorial or some other activity. They always made me nauseous. I didn't understand the source of their energy or the reason for their commitment; now I do. For whatever reason, they felt passionate about class activities when I didn't have that passion. Now, I find that I, too, have passion. I love being part of a group of people that is willing to truly listen to my ideas and help me with them, so I am willing to send out reminders of upcoming meetings and offer my home when others seem hesitant.

In my TAWL group, there is no one glue person; the role seems to be distributed across a few members. When I am overwhelmed with other facets of my life, Mary or Sara or another group member volunteers to take notes or host the next meeting. The distributed role keeps our group going; perhaps you will assume some 'glueness' when your group needs it.

Mostly, the group needs honesty. Once, as our TAWL group was winding down for the year, we sat at the picnic table in my yard and I thought I would never see the group together again. We seemed to have spent the past few meetings complaining about other people in the district and less focused on our work with children; we weren't reading or writing together. I wanted to tell the group that my needs weren't being met and invite them to talk about their views on this. Finally, and rather awkwardly, I decided to express my thoughts.

"I'm sort of frustrated with the group because our last few meetings have been gripe sessions and not particularly productive," I said, rather nervously. This was not something that I found easy to express, although I knew it was important in order to understand what the group wanted to do. Were we heading in different directions? What did I want to do about it?

After the uncomfortable silence passed, others also expressed concern. One member suggested we brainstorm areas we wanted to know more about and then use the resources of the group to decide on some readings or presentations at our meetings next year. We had a considerable list, and now we are focused, busily reading and dealing with issues within the readings as they appear (or don't) in our own classrooms. This group has been reading and talking together for a long time (3 years).

Forming a support group might take considerable time, involving a development of trust and sense of commitment and passion. The group works to respond to each others' ideas. I believe in the power of the group and have been honest with myself, knowing I need a high level of trust before I can share my writing with a group. We are forming relationships over time. They are relationships based in our reading, speaking, listening, thinking, sharing, and risking together. The order of these may vary in your group. Writing, for our group, came last. That's because we are reluctant to write; we've had unhappy experiences as writers. When we risk telling the horror stories of our writing pasts, we learn to risk more and eventually share our writing. This is part of the honesty and the relationships we are developing.

The importance, difficulty, and intensity of our writing demands that we find a support group or network that will honor our efforts, our thinking, and our pieces of writing. Whether or not this can happen at the school at which you teach, or the school you attend as a preservice teacher, depends on many things, such as: the leadership at the school or in the class, the glue person (who works to hold things together), and your relationships with your colleagues. You may not find this in your school building or the courses for which you registered, but you can find it somewhere. Before you do, you need to understand the radical nature of such groups.

IS THIS RADICAL WORK?

Finding or creating support systems can be a disruptive activity because it involves us as thinkers, a role not commonly thought of as related to being a teacher. As more teachers and preservice teachers become increasingly thoughtful, we change what happens in our lives and in the schools in which we teach. Thinking teachers are a radical group.

Teachers and preservice teachers are not typically the most politically active members of our communities. Most consider their work as focusing on children and don't see political implications in that. But, teachers as writers—which means teachers as thinkers—can be a threatening lot. We threaten basal companies (Shannon, 1989, 1990), principals, and even Boards of Education when we become thoughtful by organizing in groups. Linda Hogan (1987) asked, "Why is it that telling our lives is a subversive thing to do?" (p. 243).

It's subversive because it changes who we are, how we see, and our intentions in our work. We become more focused, more systematic, and more eager. We become less willing to take at face value the words, ideas, and recommendations of those who are far from our classrooms. We feel empowered by understanding ourselves and by the knowledge that we are not alone. Teaching is often described as a lonely profession because the adult-teacher is with children all day. This offers the adult the opportunity for many types of growth, but the lack of interaction with other adults limits growth in certain areas. A teacher's writing support group complements the teacher's life and enables him or her to clarify her thinking and subsequent (and sometimes subversive) action.

Not all groups are politically active or even specific about being political, but their existence may threaten individuals within the educational establishment. If you join a group that is exciting and seems to be doing work that is important and you find that the group encounters difficulty, the problem might be pressure from the established educational community to maintain things the way they have always been. Of course, things have not always been the way they are, but some individuals are easily threatened.

Interestingly, and rather exciting, too, some districts are cultivating change within their schools by encouraging teachers to form study groups. These districts may allow or even support teachers in choosing to teach reading in a particular way, designing their own math (or other area) programs, forming their own agendas when making decisions about staff development days, using study groups, and so on. This is an exciting change and may indicate to you that the district supports innovative thinking (a good thing to look for if you are job hunting).

What, then, are some specific possibilities for support systems for us as writers? The following sections offer some. You may invent yourself as a writer within one of these, or you may have to invent the system in which you invent yourself. Either one would be a great story. I hope you write it.

SCHOOLS AS SUPPORT STRUCTURES

I know that schools, both elementary schools in which teachers work and colleges in which we take courses as inservice and preservice teachers, are not necessarily supportive places for adult writers. Let's consider higher education first. As college or university students, our view of our own schooling may be disowned. By *disowned*, I mean that we are more focused on someone else's demands than on ourselves as learners and writers. How often have we wondered, "What does this instructor want from me? What hoops do I have to jump through to be done with this course?" We don't always feel a connection between our courses and our present or anticipated teaching experiences.

We need to search out experiences in higher education that ignite our passion and help us feel the urgency of our work. Such experiences acknowledge the importance of our work and make it feel like a contribution that we want to share with others via some type of presentation: writing, singing, talking, oral reminiscing, and more. We need to find supportive courses by talking to colleagues, interviewing instructors before we take their courses, asking for syllabi to see how instructors present their courses, and trying to tap that underground source of information that floats invisibly around colleges and universities. Find out who knows about instructors and courses and register for courses that will support you. Also, find out the last day to add or drop courses so that you can shop around even once the term has started.

Turning now to elementary schools, it seems to make sense that a group of people who come together each day for the sake of children would be interested in studying and writing about the lives of people in school. They could include inservice teachers as well as preservice teachers in practicum courses and student teaching. Vito Perrone (1991) said:

> Schools need to promote and support passion of this kind. Teachers need opportunities to reflect on their learning, on how they first came to the interests they possess and how to revitalize those interests. This suggests the need for schools to be settings where teachers share their learning with each other, read together, and have opportunities for writing and further study. The school needs to be a center of inquiry, an intellectually oriented place. (p. 117)

But how do we do this? Many schools seem stuck in a culture that will not change; they seem to perpetuate mediocrity (Sarason, 1971). Although the school is not typically the site of support for teacher writing and thinking, there are examples of schools or small groups of teachers (Klassen & Short, 1991) that cultivate themselves as such, with the support of someone present who has a writer's and researcher's vision. Although I have never experienced such a setting when I was teachering in elementary schools, I have found examples in others' work. Teachers and researchers who are publishing their stories offer us many possibilities. For example, Shirley Brice Heath (1983) worked with teachers to support their thinking and writing about the lives of their students and the communities in which those students live. Reading about the teachers with whom she worked is inspiring. She found that the teachers involved with her study were "learning researchers, who used knowledge from ethnographies of communication to build a two-way channel between communities and their classrooms" (p. 354). The teachers were a community of researchers who worked together to understand and cultivate their teaching lives. Heath played many important roles in the work. Relevant to this chapter is her role of glue as she held the group together by organizing meetings, working with collected data, and dealing with the many issues related to writing a story that portrays a community as accurately as possible. She discussed "the catalytic effect my presence in the communities and schools had for their behavior and attitude changes in the 1970s" (p. 256).

Sadly, Heath's departure from the area, after 10 years of work there, was probably one of the reasons for the teachers terminating their research and writing. The teachers lost a cohesive force. It's hard for us to change our habits or views of school life. When a dynamic leader leaves, things may lose their momentum. Fortunately, we do have other possibilities for support systems, although some may not be as conveniently located as the schools in which we teach, do our practica, student teach, or take courses. A few of these possibilities are discussed in the next section.

THE NATIONAL WRITING PROJECT

The National Writing Project (NWP) started as the Bay Area Writing Project in the early 1970s. The basic premise of the Project is that teachers will develop quality writing programs for children when those teachers develop their own writing. The Project became national and now virtually every state has a statewide writing project that is connected to NWP. In Nebraska, for example, teachers spend 5 weeks in the summer, meeting 6 hours a day to write, share, think, read, listen to speakers who are authors, and study authors and authoring. They learn the importance of writing their stories and those of their students; they leave enriched and invigorated. Sounds good, doesn't it?

David Wilson (1994) described and analyzed the lives of teachers following their participation in the NWP. The teachers he studied became "readers for their students, responding positively and specifically to their efforts, creating atmospheres that encouraged and affirmed those efforts" (p. 66). The NWP changed the teachers and their classrooms.

But not easily. Wilson also described "points of dissonance" (p. 99) that teachers have to face when they want to change their classrooms to be reflective of their personal lived experiences as writers in the NWP. Teachers need time, support, "opportunities to reflect" (p. 99) and change their ideas, and still it is not easy to change. Wilson suggested that:

> it may be that teachers will have to live with such dissonance until they are able to reconceptualize their roles as teachers or their notions of what it means to teach writing as a "process." We can help them do that by provoking and supporting them to articulate and examine their personal constructs. (p. 105)

Poignantly, Wilson wrote that change, even in a supportive and caring atmosphere, is a personal, arduous, and laborious job:

> Teachers are complex human beings, not passive receptors of knowledge. We filter experiences, like the writing project, through complicated meaning systems of personal constructs based on elements like prior experience, individual identity, and perceived social context. Our development and change, then, is messy and idiosyncratic; it reflects a mix of affect and cognition. (p. 100)

So, even as part of a support group, we need to recognize that writing our stories, changing our views about the importance of such writing, and eventually bringing our newly invented ideas about literacy into our classrooms is hard work.

Bonnie Sunstein (1994) described the culture that teachers cocreated in a 3-week writing project in New Hampshire. She found, as did Wilson, that teachers want an arena in which to work hard at understanding their stories, their lived experiences. Sunstein confirmed some of what I discussed earlier about the oppressive nature of school. She offered this explanation for what support gives teachers in groups like the National Writing Project:

> The summer program, in Tom Newkirk's words on the first day, simply "honors the teacher." It allows for personal reading and writing; it offers simply time. The culture in school does not. Teachers can tell the stories here that they can't tell in a school culture that oppresses them. They can revise themselves as writers, readers, and as teachers. The program does not transform. Rather, it affirms. (p. 233)

We need support groups that honor us, allow us time, let us tell our stories, cultivate and don't oppress, and allow us to revise ourselves. That kind of affirmation keeps us alive, interested, motivated, committed, and passionate about our work with children.

OTHER GROUPS OF EDUCATORS

If you are far from a National Writing Project site, there are other possibilities to support your work. Perrone (1991) discussed empowering teachers "particularly in relation to the active teacher [participating in] reading groups within and among schools ... and the child study movement, with its attention to teacher research" (p. 80). As Dean at the Center for Teaching & Learning, he supported the formation of the North Dakota Study Group on Evaluation at the University of North Dakota. The Study Group researched and wrote about issues of evaluation that focus on the child, the teacher, the classroom, the school, the system, and the state (see Carini, 1979, 1982). Your support group may take a collective direction, focusing on a specific issue similar to the North Dakota group's focus on evaluation, that is important to all members. Such a collective focus can be dramatic because, for example, when the group begins to read, many individuals read different things. This frames the work broadly (at first), with great depth and power. A collective focus can also intensify the analyses in which the group engages.

National organizations can sometimes be helpful in linking groups of interested educators. The most active in this respect, from my experience, is the Whole Language Umbrella. The Umbrella encourages and relies on small groups across the world called *TAWL* (Teachers Applying Whole Language) *groups.* These groups read, think, and support each others' writing. The International Reading Association sponsors local groups of teachers interested in forming reading groups. These can extend into writing support groups at the participants' discretion.

By far, the most powerful groups for support of teachers as readers and writers seem to be local individuals who are highly motivated to have such groups. Heath was already discussed. Let's look at a few other possibilities to give a sense of the broad repertoire of support systems; there are more being invented all the time. In Tucson, Kathy Short works with a few small groups, encouraging and participating with them in their research endeavors. The book *Teachers Are Researchers: Reflection and Action* (Patterson, Santa, Short, & Smith, 1993) is a collection of writings that focus on teachers doing research—telling stories through systematic collection, thinking and writing. Gordon Wells (1994) also worked with teachers to publish his edited volume, *Changing Schools From Within: Creating Communities of Inquiry.* You could write a book with your colleagues about your experiences at practicum sites, in student teaching, and in your own classrooms.

Marilyn Cochran-Smith and Susan Lytle (1993) are avid supporters and co-inquirers with teachers who are researching into and writing about their lives in classrooms. They described teacher research projects in which teachers tell their stories; they also questioned the place and nature of this work:

> The most fundamental issue is whether teacher research will remain on the fringe of educational reform or whether it will be at the forefront. Our argument is that communities for teacher research—communities with particular ways of organizing time, using talk, constructing texts, and interpreting the tasks of teaching and schooling—have the potential to move teacher research from fringe to forefront by fostering reforms that amount to more than tinkering with or reinforcing existing structures. Communities of teacher researchers can play an essential role in school reform. Not only does their work add to the knowledge base on teaching, but their collective power as knowledge-generating communities also influences broader

school policies regarding curriculum, assessment, school organization, and home–school linkages. Through teacher-research communities, teachers' voices play a more prominent part in the dialogue of school reform. (p. 103)

Brenda Power and Ruth Hubbard are coediting a journal for teacher researchers appropriately entitled, *Teacher Research.* The journal is an outlet for teachers to publish and read each others' work. They also wrote a book (Hubbard & Power, 1993) that offers ways of choosing a question, strategies for collecting and analyzing data, and instruction on how to write up research. The chapter entitled 'You Are Not Alone' suggested ways to obtain funding for your research. They also discussed support groups:

> The importance of having a community of colleagues who are teacher-researchers [storytellers] cannot be overemphasized. This community may be as local as your own school or as far-flung as a few key teacher-researchers you find in journals and texts. But you do need someone, somewhere, who can help you develop ideas. You need to have people you trust to read or listen to your research proposals, to critique your design and budget plans, and to encourage you to try and try again when a proposal is rejected. (p. 131)

Efforts at becoming a support group and distributing writing can be repeated in any locale. In Lincoln, Nebraska, a group of teachers decided to publish a book through the district office. That office will pay for copying and paper so that the group can share their stories with others in the district. At the time of this writing, we are considering proposing our efforts to a publishing house to reach even more colleagues. It's exciting (and scary) work. One of the teachers who is in this group asks, "Can I put in how frustrated I've been about trying to change but not feeling like I know enough?"

"Ohh, this scares me," says another. "Can't I do it with Kim [her colleague]?" She decides that perhaps she can write a chapter if she is a coauthor. The questions, decisions, excitement, frustration, curiosity, and multitude of other feelings have begun to emerge. We are becoming a group—still in its fragile and vulnerable state; it has taken months to make the decision to get together to talk about what we might want to do. Once we are together, the ideas and questions flood our meetings. We took an important step in our journey together by committing ourselves publicly—out loud— to writing and being supportive of each other's writing. No one in our group is the glue yet. Understanding who the glue is, though, will be important for our survival as a writers' support group.

Anne Dyson (1993) studies young children's written language development. She made the argument that young writers develop *neighborhoods* in which they write. The kids move into a particular area of the classroom, establish relationships with their neighbors, learn to live and work together, and, within the many layers of that context, they write. Our support groups need to feel like neighborhoods in which we want to grow up as writers. When I think back to my own neighborhood, summer evenings come to mind. We played hard all day, but nights seemed to revitalize us with new energy. We'd play hiding and finding games, have races, and play kickball. Our voices seemed different and the sound traveled differently than during the day. I knew that neighborhood. I knew what I was safe doing and what would get me in trouble. I knew the people, the places, and the activities.

We need safe neighborhoods when we seek support groups. We need to be able to be who we are, be able to stretch who we are, to revise ourselves. And all this needs to occur within a safety that allows us to grow. Study your writing neighborhood as you study yourself and your students. Make sure it is a good place for you to be. Risk carefully and respect the confidential nature of everything that happens within your group.

SUSTAINING THE GROUP

Writers' support groups need different things for sustenance, depending on the individuals involved and their specific needs. If a group seems to be working for those involved, we cannot rely solely on some kind of inertia for it to stay in motion. We need to exert energy to sustain a group. You might decide that beginning with a covered dish supper is an important part of 'nourishing' a group's collective activity. Perhaps you want pizza delivered or prefer a glass of wine and some cheese. I like eating with groups of people I feel safe and comfortable with.

Some individuals have spiritual needs. When I discuss a group's process, I try to understand and explain the group's energy—how does the group feel? I am honest with myself about groups and try to trust (and explain, at least to myself) my intuitive sense of a group.

Electronic connections are probably going to lead to groups who form and sustain themselves by being in touch electronically. There is much potential for regular electronic meetings because we can share our writing and concerns about our writing as well as read others' responses at our leisure—at our own inclination and as time permits. So, if I am unable to sleep some night, I can write to you and you can respond in the morning. We can also be on listservs, a way of connecting many people in electronic discussions so that they can all read each others' comments, thoughts, and responses.

As I wrote earlier, the glue of a group is important in sustaining that group. The glue might be a specific individual, a distributed responsibility, or something less visible. Some groups seem to stay together because of the energy between the individuals and the intensely productive group process that develops. Some groups stay together because of their philosophical connection; we feel supported when we immerse ourselves in a group beliefs similar to our own about teaching, language, learning, and curriculum. Again, trust your intuition. If a group feels right, it may be a place to write.

If you are lucky enough to be doing coursework in a class that develops into a support group, you will find it a challenge to maintain that group after the course ends. The TAWL group I am involved with grew out of a class some folks didn't want to end. Of the 25 class members, about 3 have remained with the group for the past 3 years and are still members. We have accumulated others along the way, developing a process that rests in our safety, comfort, passion, motivation, and commitment.

YOU'LL BE DIFFERENT

You are different when you are a writer in a support group. You venture into yourself and others in a way that is not characteristic in most schools or social settings. At times, you may venture out and express yourself in the teachers' lounge or at a meeting. Such expressions of self are bold statements and sometimes lead to finding others who believe as you do—an exciting thing. Other times, you may feel ostracized or embarrassed. Writing and gathering support for your writing are powerful activities. You uncover much of who you are and how you view the world. It is important work that changes you, as you clarify and create yourself. It is admirable work and will affect every child you teach because you will gain the sensitivity, clarity, confusion, concern, caring, and angst of being a writer.

chapter 5

Framing Our Stories

I submit that learning is relational, that it can occur only in the context of a relationship and that a relationship cannot occur unless those involved with it consciously commit themselves to it. This conscious commitment condemns the fixed patterns that are the historical mode of education because the essential dynamic of a relationship insists that the self of one person communicate with the self of another person, and it means that neither person withholds the participating self. The existentialist argues that a person is a meaning-disclosing being, and it is that shared commitment to self-disclosure that unifies the student–teacher and learning–teaching relationships. Thus, the self of the teacher is as central to the development of the curriculum which is the environment of those relationships as is the course the "teacher" is asked to teach.

—Hope (1972, p. 110)

Any story we tell or write is framed in some way. A frame is a point of view, perspective, stance, or relationship that is a foundational part of a story. If I tell you a story about a child in school, an important part of that story is who I am. Am I the child's teacher or his or her father? Am I a literacy researcher or a lawyer? If a story is framed in such a way that I find myself responding with a high degree of intensity (anger, joy, frustration, etc.), then I look at myself first and try to understand why there is energy between the story being told and my own story. This is the relational part of learning that Scott Hope mentioned in the opening quote.

Because our stories are relational, they are unique. The participants in any relationship make that relationship unique. This is my understanding of Hope's use of the phrase "shared commitment to self-disclosure." When a teacher tells a story, that story is one part of the relationships between all the players in the story. It is from the teacher's frame and is self-disclosing, whether or not we state that we are self-disclosing. When I tell a story that seems like a superficial summary of a situation, I am not disclosing much about the story or myself. When I tell a story with passion, commitment, motivation, and intensity, I am telling a lot about the story and myself and I am taking a risk, making myself vulnerable, and asserting who I am.

Frames can lead to scholarly arguments or not-so-scholarly arguments. The closer our frames are to our own hearts, the closer they come to making us vulnerable. As a result, some stories are quite stirring as they paint pictures of the inequities, injustices, and actions we find immoral.

For example, in Denny Taylor's (1991) book, *Learning Denied*, she told the story of Patrick's life in and out of school during his primary years. Many tests were administered to Patrick and it was determined that he had "learning problems" (p. 6). The school framed Patrick as an atypical learner in need of help, and believed he needed to begin some sort of remedial education as soon as possible. Taylor's frame was that tests are limiting and give a reduced view of what a child can do. She used, instead, an in-depth study of his literacy called a *biographic literacy profile* to gain an understanding of the broad repertoire of literacy activity in which Patrick participated and succeeded.

So who is right? Is Patrick to be labeled and placed in some sort of remedial program focusing on what he is lacking, or is he unique and in need of an educational setting that cultivates his uniqueness? This poignant story is painful to read. Patrick's case went through various meetings and hearings at which voices were raised and many tears were shed. Finally, Patrick's parents decide to withdraw him from the school because his needs were not being met. Taylor helped them develop a program of learning at home so that Patrick's self-esteem could be supported as he learned. She reported that after a few years, Patrick was reading and writing more than many typical middle school children, and he returned to the public school setting.

Patrick's story has many frames. The way individuals framed the story led to various decisions being made and actions taken. The teachers and other school officials certainly believed that they knew what Patrick needed and that he could be served within the school. Their frame was constructed by the school's program and procedures. His parents, with the help of Taylor, framed Patrick as a learner who was being thwarted in the school setting. They found much support for making their difficult decision to remove him from school for a few years. Taylor, as the researcher and author of the piece, framed the story in a very important way. She wanted the reader to understand that a child's performance in school may not reflect the full repertoire of the child's literacy possibilities. The book inspires discussion and further research.

Frames, then, are not merely molded and used. They are points of view that reflect decision making, many hours of thinking, and a melding of other people's work through our own understanding and experience and the very core of who we are. In this chapter, I discuss the self and our lived experiences as frames for our stories. Then I present ways we can develop ourselves so that our frames are informed by points of view and information outside of ourselves.

OUR LIVED EXPERIENCES
ARE OUR PRIMARY FRAMES

Making sense of the stories that unfold within our classroom means making sense of who we are, how we think about ourselves, the children we teach, and the many contexts and situations of which we are a part. Max Van Manen (1986) wrote that "[t]houghtfulness ... is a peculiar quality that has as much to do with what we are as with what we do" (p. 12). Framing our stories, then, begins with living our lives and it is our lived experiences that form our frames.

Many teachers say they leave their lives at the door of the classroom, and once they are with their students they forget about their income tax, pending divorce, car trouble, financial difficulties, or other concerns. Teaching may refocus us onto others, rather than ourselves, but we focus through who we are. We see the world through the glasses of our own experiences. Our lives—the essence of who we are—frame our way of being in the classroom and our understanding of classroom activity as much as they frame our understanding of an impending divorce, our financial problems, the beauty in a spring day, or meeting with a new lover.

Our frames are wonderfully flexible because they are within our own minds. Frank Smith (1990) explained our minds in a powerful way. He reminded us that everyone is born with a brain, but our minds are something we construct over time and experience. Our minds affect how we see. Van Manen (1986) discussed how we see through our minds' "eyes":

How does a parent or teacher *see* a child? Is there a unique pedagogical way of seeing children, different from the way other people would see them? A strange question perhaps. Given that seeing is a sensory act, don't we all see children the same way? For example, we see the same figure, the same movement, the same child skipping rope or painting a picture.

But we never see anything purely. How and what we *see* depends on who and how we are in the world. How and what we see in a child is dependent on our relationship to that child. (p. 16)

Our initial frame of any story is our own story. And our own story is 'dependent on our relationship' with those around us. Thus, a frame is quite complex, as it rests in an understanding of ourselves and our relationships. I hope that you've begun to write or tell your story by following the leads in chapter 1. Perhaps you've even started a longer story. As you make sense of your story, let your own life wrap itself around and weave itself through your story as you write or tell it. I do that with the stories in this book. The short stories I tell in chapter 2 radiate from who I am. The longer story of oral language in the classroom and how it reminds me of the occasional work I did in the factory where my father worked is another example. A storyteller's life permeates the story because the storyteller makes a conscious effort to understand the story and the self. By understanding both—the story and the storyteller—our teaching and learning lives and the lives of our students are enhanced. I acknowledge that my stories are me because that is what makes them and me so unique and important.

Sometimes the stories I live appear to conflict with who I am. That was the case when I first moved to rural New York. I didn't know much about the children's ways of living and I soon collided with a host of values and beliefs different from those I brought to my new home. By working to tell the story of the differences and similarities, I focus on learning and growing from the experiences rather than judging them from a rigid internal place. I found it encouraging that I was not the only teacher to feel like I had entered a new culture when I began my teaching career.

Herb Kohl's (1967) book, *36 Children*, is his story of becoming a teacher in Harlem. His sixth-grade class scared, excited, worried, and worked him until, by Halloween, he was so saturated with the children that he was losing his own story. Kohl wrote:

> After dinner I had to be on the streets again. It was five flights down. I reached the landing of the second floor lost in a fantasy of Harlem Halloweens. There were people talking on the ground floor, a couple saying good night to someone who had moved in, a female face. I realized how lonely I was; wanted to wait until the couple had left and then trick-or-treat myself.
>
> They left, the door was closed and I stared at it, paused, then decided that if a light was still on after I had a beer I would knock. I returned after six beers and it was on. To be true to the children and myself, I knocked. That was how I met Judy, my wife.
>
> We talked well into the night, two months of days with 6–1 poured out of me, the anguish and the hope, my own uncertainty and my confidence. All the contradictions that lived in my classroom were articulated for the first time. I showed her the children's writing, the ridiculous textbooks I had to use. Then, after it had all tumbled out, I could look at her and try to discover who she was. (pp. 52–53)

We need to tell our stories because they fill us up in some odd way that makes us feel lonely if we don't let them tumble out by telling them. The anguish, uncertainty, and contradictions give us headaches (or other ailments of the body or soul) and one way to find relief is to tell the stories. Kohl was experiencing the shock of the reality of his students' lives in the ghetto. He framed the telling of the story within his life, his development as a teacher, and his relationships with his students.

Van Manen (1986), discussing teacher burnout, suggested that:

> Teacher burnout is not necessarily a symptom of excessive effort, of being overworked. It is the condition of not knowing why we are doing what we are doing. Burnout is the evidence of helplessness, of no longer being able to find a positive answer to the sigh, "What's the use?" (p. 29)

Teacher burnout is when our stories stop because they have piled up with no outlet and our frames become narrowed and bitter. It is when we become a hamster in the exercise wheel. Unlike the hamster, we are aware that we are going nowhere while using a lot of energy. Our stories are how we make sense of what we do. Even the hamster metaphor can be meaningful when we frame it in, for example, the importance of exercise for the body and mind. Framing our stories helps us make sense of our lived experiences.

READING TO EXTEND THE SELF

The first few pages of this chapter are framed. I use my own thinking and show how my thinking was stretched by others' work. I brought Scott Hope, Denny Taylor, Herb Kohl, and Max Van Manen into the discussion because they wrote things that affected the way I think, tell stories, and approach my classroom and my research. My life experiences have changed because of my reading. So, in the telling of our stories, we can incorporate the stories that made an impression on us. For a teacher, some of those stories may be fiction and some may be nonfiction.

Are you thinking, "Oh no. He's not going to tell us that long and boring research articles are great stories that we need to read"?

I'm not. I'm suggesting that some long articles are like stories because of what unfolds within. And that some of those articles may bore you at one time in your life, but may be of intense interest when you find yourself involved in something related to the article that is relevant to your own lived experiences in your classroom. You start to read because you question how it is you know something. You may have found yourself saying that you know a certain thing to be true for your students or yourself. Reading helps you retrace that knowing.

How do we know something when we say we know it? For example, if you tell me that Maria is a good reader, how do you know that? If you are Maria's mother, perhaps you know that because you listen as she reads to another family member or friend. If you are Maria's teacher, perhaps you know that she is a good reader because she chooses books from the library that are usually read by older children and you are sure she understands what she has read because she writes elaborate responses to her reading in a literature log. If you are one type of reading specialist, you know that Maria is a good reader because you gave her a test that indicated she is reading 3 years above her grade level. If you are another type of reading specialist, you know that Maria is a good reader because you studied her as a reader in order to write a literacy profile that includes the many genres she enjoys reading, samples of her writing, and a transcription of some interviews you did with her. There are many frames for knowing something.

When I began teaching, I 'knew' how to teach reading. I passed out the basals and told each child to do many things that were clearly written out for me in the teacher's guide. I assigned worksheets and workbook pages and had children copy long poems from the chalkboard so that they would be busy while I worked with my reading groups. I knew that teaching reading involved grouping and I had groups based on ability.

As my teaching life progressed, I had experiences with children (like those described in chap. 2), and I began to read more about language development. The things I knew about teaching reading became things I knew were wrong. I was using materials that assumed that children must be taught little words and ideas before they could learn big ones. However, in my classroom experience, I found that children could read *Tyrannosaurus Rex,* but could not always read *said.* Why was this? There seemed to be tension between what the authors of the basals were saying about reading and what my students were actually doing. My interest was piqued. I wanted to know more about reading and written language development. I began to read.

My biggest problem with trying to read what others have to say about reading and writing is that I fall asleep so easily after a full day of school. I love to teach, but it is exhausting. I began to judge articles and books by a nap rating system. An article would be a one-nap piece, if I could read it and doze off for only one nap. Two-nappers are those articles that required two naps, and so on. I rarely finished anything that received more than a three-nap rating because my interest just was not sufficiently piqued.

Of course, a big chore was going to the library to dig out articles. I enjoyed learning to use new electronic methods to access information, such as ERIC. But I just didn't have the time and energy to go to the library that often.

Journals ... We Deliver

I found that I was constantly looking up articles in *Language Arts,* the journal for elementary school teachers from the National Council of Teachers of English (NCTE). More recently, *Primary Voices* has also been a journal of choice, also from NCTE, because it is edited by classroom teachers. I also like *Reading Teacher,* from the International Reading Association (IRA). I read, on the inside cover of these journals, about subscription rates. I decided to join IRA and NCTE because the journals would be delivered and I wouldn't have to go to the library as often.

Both organizations have book publishing departments. I receive lists of new books and can look for books by folks whose articles I enjoyed—all from the comfort of my napping chair. IRA and NCTE also sell your name to lots of other organizations, so you can receive information about other books and organizations. I don't love junk mail but I do relish convenience, so I subscribe. The supplemental mailings keep me informed about what other organizations and publishers are doing. The journals also give information about national and local conventions.

The editors make choices about whose articles to include in each issue. Typically, there are a broad range of people and the same names do not appear over and over again. However, there are some names that become staples, like Dorothy Watson, Ken Goodman, Yetta Goodman, Jerome Harste, Denny Taylor, Frank Smith, Kathy Short, and Luis Moll. Those whose articles I enjoy (the ones that are no-nappers) are the folks whose books I look for and are published by NCTE or IRA.

If you are taking just one course from a local university, that is the time to subscribe because your professor can sign you off as a student and you will receive the student rate. Also, membership may be tax deductible. All in all, it's quite convenient to have these delivered. I have never had an issue arrive that did not have at least one article relevant to my current interest in classroom activity. Journals also have ongoing departments such as 'the latest in children's literature', so you stay current in other facets of your teaching, not just things that are written about in feature articles.

I don't want to start sounding like an advertisement for NCTE and IRA. These organizations thrive on teachers' and researchers' scholarly and financial contributions. I'm also an active member of the Whole Language Umbrella, the most teacher-centered group with which I have ever been affiliated; their members' journal is *Talking Points*, a fine voice I highly recommend. I receive mailings from Heineman, St. Martin's Press, Stenhouse, and other publishing firms. They have exciting books that enrich our frames. Folks in Tucson, Arizona are lucky to have Debra Jacobsen as a member of their Teachers Applying Whole Language support group. Debra uses her guest house as a bookstore and stocks the latest works from a variety of publishers. A visit to Debra's house means you get to see her garden, bark along with her dogs, enjoy her company, and listen to her ideas about which books might best match your present interests. When visiting a bookstore is also visiting a friend who knows so much, it certainly becomes even more exciting and interesting to frame your stories in books and articles. Debra is writing the story of the Tucson TAWL group's origin, with a few members in someone's living room, to its present membership of more than 2,000 and a bookstore. Check out your local TAWL or other teacher support groups and other area bookstores.

How Much? How Often?

The more we read, the more we affect the frames we use to understand children's learning and our role in it. How do we know how often to read or how much? This depends on who you are. It brings me back to the first chapter of this book and the importance of knowing your own literate life and how it overflows into your classroom. Read because of who you are and to enhance the stories of the literate lives in the classrooms where you work with children. If you are like me, you will always feel like there is something else you should be reading. Some friends of mine wear shirts that say "So many books, so little time." That's how I feel. Pace yourself to support your thirst to know but not drown yourself.

Read more of the people you like. This is what we tell our students in elementary schools. It's what I do, too. I read one of Roal Dahl's books to my second-grade class. Then, while in the media center, one child found another of his books. The children asked me to read that to the class, too. We were gorging on Dahl's work. I do the same with writers of books and articles about children's literacy development. I read more of those whose style and content I love. Find whose work you love and feast upon it.

THE LIVED EXPERIENCES OF OTHERS
AFFECT OUR FRAMES

Our own lived experiences are our primary influences, and the lives of others may impact us via fine books that are becoming popular among educators.

Reading Others' Short Stories

Collections of short stories can be found in a variety of places. As I previously discussed, journal articles can seem like short stories when they are interesting to us. There is another recent source of short stories that I have come to enjoy. Teachers are gathering together to write books. Orin Cochrane and Ethel Buchanan (1993) brought together 16 stories of teachers of various grade levels all describing how they begin their school year in whole language classrooms. This book is an easy read because of the low number of pages in each chapter and because of the variety of voices—we hear from 16 teachers all telling their stories in their own voices. There are also photos and samples of children's writing.

Teachers are expressing their curiosities and findings in other volumes, too. Gordon Wells (1994) and 11 teachers discussed how they are "changing schools from within" in a book by that name. The teachers in this book told of specific research questions they had and how they addressed them in their classrooms. The various topics include: children's journals, oral language in the classroom, the roles of teachers, and English as a second language. They wrote about what made them curious about an issue and then presented some of the reading they did to make sense of their question. Each one discussed a research question that emerged from their curiosity and how they did research in their classrooms.

Other editors are collecting teachers' short stories, too. One of my favorite collections is called *Teachers are Researchers: Reflection and Action* (edited by Patterson, Santa, Short, & Smith, 1993). Here, teachers from various grade levels, including the university, tell their framed stories. One of my favorites is Caryl Crowell's (1993) story of her third-grade children dealing with Desert Storm, the military action in the Middle East. The children had many questions and pursued them vigorously. Caryl acted as a support for the children's learning and also kept track of their growth and changes during their study. By the time they had finished their study, the children had abandoned playing war on the playground, read about wars and the holocaust, and gained insights into living together as a peaceful community. Caryl told the story of her students in their own pursuit of understanding the horrors and tragedy of war. That story is framed by the realities of war, the interactions among her children, the children's voices, and the classroom community's reading about war and history. Caryl's understanding of language, literacy, history, and current events were stretched by the activities that took place in her classroom.

Teachers who are serious about framing their stories, and subsequently presenting them, are researchers. You are a researcher when you write your literacy autobiography. You are doing research into yourself. Then, you become a researcher into other situations—in classrooms—with the clarity you gain from studying yourself.

Reading Longer Stories

It takes time to read longer stories written by others. They are usually written by researchers who have the time to do such extensive writing and the library work necessary to frame these pieces. There are some fascinating longer stories available. These are not scientific reports in the way you might think. They are longer and more scholarly, but they are not loaded with statistical analyses that are unreadable by most.

For example, in *Learning Denied*, Taylor told the story of Patrick that I discussed earlier. Taylor wrote another book with Catherine Dorsey-Gaines (*Growing Up Literate: Learning from Inner-City Families,* 1988) in which they described the literacy lives of families in the inner city. *Growing up Literate* is a heart-wrenching story, framed by the work of the Children's Defense Fund as well as the work of many literacy researchers. Teachers reading *Growing Up Literate* will never be the same. The book evokes important questions about literacy, such as: What is the whole picture of my students' literacy? What have I been missing by limiting myself to their lives in school?

Perhaps you noticed that I read and referred to two books by Taylor. She is one author whose works I have gorged on. I look forward to her articles and books. I rejoiced when she shared her own literacy autobiography with me (and all of the other readers of *The Reading Teacher* [Taylor, 1993b]) because it was an affirmation of the importance of telling our own stories.

Longer stories can change the way we look at our own classrooms. In *School Children At-Risk*, Virginia Richardson, Ursula Casanova, Peggy Placier, and Karen Guilfoyle (1989) showed that learning disabilities are contextually driven. This means that one child might be learning disabled in one classroom but not in another. This is a challenge to the claim that we can objectively determine that a child is learning disabled. It means we need to understand the settings in which children learn. I personalize this research when I use it to frame my understanding of children's lives in school.

Some of these longer stories are being written by educational anthropologists or sociologists who view situations as cultures that demand description and interpretation. You may see some of these referred to as *ethnographies* when written by anthropologists. An example may demonstrate more clearly the power of a longer story. Valerie Polakow teaches and researches at Eastern Michigan University. She recently described the lives of single mothers and their children in what she called *the other America* (Polakow, 1993). Her descriptions are powerful and the political and economic interpretations that she presented are inspirational for those of us who advocate for quality opportunities for children in school.

Polakow described Heather, a second grader. In this excerpt, the words in quotes are Heather's teacher's and those out of quotes are Polakow's:

> "This child just does not know the difference between right and wrong—she absolutely does not belong in a normal classroom with normal children." I look at Heather, now being sent to the principal's office, awkwardly slipping in her flipflops three sizes too big for her, walking down the corridor—in the middle of a snowy December—dressed in a summer blouse several sizes too small and a long flimsy skirt. What had Heather done? "I've given up on this child—she's socially dysfunctional—three times now we've caught her stealing free lunch and storing it in her desk to take home! (p. 138)

Polakow researched to find out why Heather was stealing food. The food stamps ran out by the weekend and the little bit of food Heather stole helped sustain the children in her family until the following week.

This is a powerful story. It is one that comes to light when a researcher has the time and energy, commitment, passion, and motivation to understand the why and how of a situation. These findings help every one of us as teachers; they give us cause to stop and think about what is happening to the children we teach with and learn from. It affects how we frame the stories unfolding daily in our classrooms.

We then frame our stories from the frames of others' stories. Like looking in the mirror when there is a mirror behind, we see infinite possibilities. When I read some stories, I find that I resonate with them. They seem just the stories I need to be reading for where I am in my development as a teacher at a given time.

EXPERIENCES BEYOND READING

We need not only read to share in the lives of others. Included here are a few of the many other possibilities.

Conventions

Attending conventions is a powerful way to feed the part of you that wants to frame stories with a fuller perspective. Conventions are typically annual occurrences of the organizations I previously mentioned; they also have local conventions run by local councils or groups. Most of the people attending these are there by choice, so the mood is usually friendly and focused. I like both the collegiality and the intensity because it's an opportunity to talk and think. I also get to meet, question, and talk with some of the people whose work I've read. It's fun to combine a face and personality with some of the frames we read.

Courses

Obviously, college or university courses are places where we can challenge our thinking and examine our frames. Or are they? Whenever possible, shop around for a course that allows your voice, your frame, to be part of the course. Look for instructors who value where you are in your thinking and want to challenge you, too.

BEING SOCIAL BEINGS

Cyril Houle (1961) wrote that we, as adults, learn for one of three reasons. First, we might learn because we have a thirst to know things and to play with ideas. Second, we might learn because our learning will help us achieve a goal (like an increase in salary). Third, some of us learn because we like being around people; we like the social nature of learning. Whether or not we like people, teachers' learning has a social side to it. Framing our stories is a social activity that is not always accepted by those in our social situations. Some teachers may be in schools where colleagues are not interested in sharing learning and ideas. Others might be more interested in life outside of school, rather than dealing with stories from within. Teaching in some schools is a lonely business. Framing stories can be a social occasion, something that may be difficult in some schools. It is important to find people who will listen to you, support you, and push your thinking as you frame your stories. I discussed support systems in chapter 4.

Live Your Life

My final bit of advice is to live a rich and full life. Relish in beautiful sunsets. Dance along the seashore. Trick or treat in your apartment building. Be true to who you are and what calls you. I am constantly struggling with this. I have a passion for writing and so I write a lot. Yet as I sit here on a sunny November day, I know that the weeks ahead will mean cold and snowy weather in Nebraska. I should be outside walking in leaves and smelling the smells of autumn. Still, here I sit and write. I have made a commitment to me and to you to write this book. So write I will. And as I do, the day slips away and I find myself picturing someone reading this book outside on a day like today, or by a warm wood stove in Vermont, or at a kitchen table surrounded by the remnants of the Sunday paper. Once again, it is by coming to terms with myself that I find my motivation, passion, and commitment. My writing is an essential part of my lived experience.

Our lived experiences frame our stories. That living and framing include writing inside when it is lovely outside; they include not writing; they include losing ourselves in the events of our classrooms; and they include a long weekend away from our classrooms—in the garden, by the ocean, near a stream, or in the desert, or wherever it is that we let ourselves explore what we are creating—in our minds. Our frames are made of our relationships with ourselves and our students. Framing our stories means understanding who we are and being sensitive to and respectful of who we are. Framing also means being open to the voices in books, articles, and presentations. The frames for the stories that unfold in our classrooms provide us with insights into understanding and move us toward the goal of creating classrooms that uncover the hidden possibilities for our students.

FRAMING THE STORIES WE TELL AND WRITE

The discussion of framing in this chapter relates to how we know what we know. The various ways of framing our stories are ways of validating our stories with and through the work of others. Sometimes, what we read may appear to invalidate our stories. I'm not too quick to let this happen. I prefer to keep searching for frames that confirm what I am thinking. And, to avoid sounding too consistent, I also like to have my thinking challenged, so I read different-from-me frames and try my hand at scholarly arguments to explore the soundness of my own thinking.

The important point of framing is that it is used in the telling and writing of our stories. We bring in the voices of others to confirm our own voice. Or, we might bring in the voices of others to show that we are thinking differently from them. Either way, the voices of others help us. They may help us by confirming our own voices or they may help us by forcing us to articulate arguments against another.

I sometimes challenge the teachers with whom I work, research, learn, and tell stories. Periodically, one of them will say, "Research shows us that ..." and I quickly ask, "Which research? Who says that?" I want to know who they are reading and how that reading is framing their views of teaching and learning. We feel comfortable enough with each other to challenge one another this way. We push each other in our thinking as we read and listen to each others' stories. We suggest to each other things we may want to read and incorporate into the stories we are working on. I close this chapter with a story framed in years of teaching, my growing understanding of rural children in the other America, and the importance of trying to see from the child's point of view.

THE CHILD'S POINT OF VIEW

My second-grade classroom was a typical primary classroom. It was a large box with square floor space, and one bathroom in the corner. Over the years, we had many discussions about the bathroom at our class meetings. These discussions included boys leaving the seat up, boys wetting the seat, someone writing words on the walls, putting paper towels in the toilet, leaving the water at the sink running, and privacy. The door did not have a lock, so when the stop sign was turned to *stop* we knew to wait politely. Knocking was considered a rude interruption.

Amy spent many long periods of time in the bathroom. This created an anxious situation for me, her teacher. Once I asked her, "Do you feel sick?"

She answered, "No."

"Well," I said, "You spend so long in the bathroom, I thought you might be ill."

"No, I'm okay," she assured me.

Not too many days later, Amy was once again in the bathroom. A small parade of children was going to the bathroom door, realizing that the stop sign was showing, and returning anxiously to their seats. I walked over to the bathroom door and leaned my ear close to it. I don't know what I was expecting to hear; it's just one of those things I found myself doing as a teacher.

I heard the water running so I decided to gently knock on the door.

"Come in," was Amy's reply.

I was a little surprised at the invitation because I thought that she was on the toilet. I had backed myself into a precarious situation by knocking. I opened the door very slowly and, hearing the water running, I looked in at Amy, feeling all the eyes of the classroom on my back.

Amy was standing at the sink with her hands under the running water. She must have seen the question in my eyes, because before I could ask what she was doing, Amy asked, "Mr. Meyer, how do they do that?"

"How do they do what?"

"How do they make the water come out warm?"

We were living in a tiny town where some kids had dirt floors, wood stoves for heat, and no hot running water. I knew Amy's home had electricity because I passed it each day and saw lights on. I didn't know there was no hot water heater. Later in the day, we walked to the large closet that housed the hot water heater for our building. I explained it to Amy.

Amy's view of the world changed and so did mine. As I write stories about children and teachers now, I try to get at what they are feeling, thinking, and understanding through the lens of what I am feeling, thinking and understanding. There is a constant tension there because even as an adult I sometimes find myself wondering why everyone's view of the world is not the same as mine. The challenge for us is to live our lives as teachers and learners in classrooms where we pay careful attention to who is there, the richness and uniqueness of their lives, and the importance of honoring them. Taylor (1993a) wrote:

> In studies of reading and writing that so often begin with words, children are unknown, and the circumstances of their everyday lives are unspecified. Lost in anonymity, their faces are masked by categorized conditions on which educational researchers have focused their attention. Under these circumstances, teachers have no way of speaking about literacy and the lives of children. But what happens if the child is unmasked? What happens if instead of beginning with *words* teachers are given the opportunity to begin with the *child?* (p. 145)

Here, then, is the challenge for us. We must find those children or areas about which we feel passionate, motivated, and committed to act. Then, find other voices that support (or don't support) us in our thinking. Then, weave those voices throughout the stories we want to tell of the children we know and love. Teachers who can frame the stories they tell express their commitment, motivation, and passion. We frame the stories from our point of view and from our understanding of the children's points of view, thus gaining insights into their lived experiences. We include all the relevant voices we can find as a way of articulating mutuality (our lives are built together) and understanding. It's not easy to frame stories; it feels awkward expressing our knowledge or understanding, and we may even feel pedantic when we talk about Dewey, Vygotsky, or Piaget. Keep in mind that writing stories and framing them is one of the most professional and responsible acts a teacher can commit.

chapter 6

I Liked Reading This Book, But I Still Haven't Written a Thing

Wilbur never forgot Charlotte. Although he loved her children and grandchildren dearly, none of the new spiders ever quite took her place in his heart. She was in a class by herself. It is not often someone comes along who is a true friend and a good writer. Charlotte was both.

—White (1952, p. 184)

My second-grade class sat on the floor as I read the last two chapters of *Charlotte's Web*. They cried. I cried. They saw me cry. Charlotte was dead. I looked around the circle of listening children. Franklin, who is always so strong and reminds us of spiders sometimes because he climbs the side of the school building to get balls off of the roof (much to the chagrin of the playground staff), sat with his knees drawn up to his chest. Gracie's tears streamed down her cheeks. Melissa's wide smile was one, with her bottom lip quivering a bit. No one spoke. We can hear the bubbling of the aquarium filter, the leaves pushing against the window on this dreary, rainy autumn day, and the hum of the classroom lights.

Theresa has moved over, as she often does during the time we spend listening to books, and put her head on the lap of the person next to her. She was two people away from me and was intent upon my face. Perhaps she noticed my tears. "I've read this book so many times," I finally said, "and each time I reach the end, I cry."

There was silence again. The children are, I believe, soaking in the story the way we soak in a warm bath. It surrounds us, we are submerged. I decided, quietly to myself, as I looked around the circle, that this is what Frank Smith (1988) meant by the *literacy club*. We are readers and writers and we are in a unique literacy club. It is the one we cultivate together in our classroom. I know this because I know the time that we spend listening to stories is different when one person is missing or when we have a visitor. Our literacy club is sensitive to every member.

Theresa moved her head ever so slightly, enough so that I sensed she was going to say something. I looked at her and smiled. "Mr. Meyer," she began, "You have white hairs in your beard."

Needless to say, I was quite surprised. Was one of the members of our club not "in" in quite the way I had been imagining? Surely, she felt the ending of this story as it saturated the room.

"Theresa, I guess I'm just getting old."

Suddenly it struck me that perhaps she had made a connection to aging and dying and she feared for my life. At the same time, I wondered if I was flattering myself a bit too much by thinking she put all this together because of the intensity of her membership in our literacy club.

"Why did you notice my beard?" I asked.

"I just never noticed your white hairs before."

I was faced with a hard decision at this point. Theresa, whether or not she knows it, provided a segue into a related area of discussion. We could have begun discussing deaths we had known, or fear, or are anticipating.

"Any other thoughts about this book, now that we're done hearing it together?" I asked.

"I knew she was going to die," said Tom.

"I saw the tape," said Melinda.

"Me, too," came many echoes.

"We own it," said Jessica.

"I know a lot of you have seen it and I've read it before, too, so I knew Charlotte would die in the end," I say. "It's funny, though, each time that I read it, I just don't want it to end that way."

"I know what you mean," said Loma.

Once again we were discussing a book, our feelings, our lives. The children discussed grandparents and other relatives who had died. Some of them talked about heroes and heroines. Eventually myths arose, like the story about the boys who died at the shopping mall before it was built. We cover a lot of ground as we live our literate lives together.

And we'll write. We'll all write. Some of our stories will sound like *Charlotte's Web* and some will even use the same characters. Some of us will write about close and caring friends, others will write about loneliness. Some of us will struggle with our writing and others will write page after page after page and not want to stop for math, music, art, or other special classes. We are motivated to write because of our classroom setting. But now, I leave the classroom and turn to you, the reader.

This chapter is for the reader who has difficulty initiating his or her own writing. In other words, as the chapter name says quite blatantly, you've read the book up until here, hopefully enjoyed it, but you have not written a thing. In chapter 1, I made a case for writing our own stories, specifically the story of your literate life. I hope that you read that chapter and that you have given yourself the time to think about your literate life. You can think about it in the shower, in a car, on a walk, or during a boring television show. If you haven't written anything yet, perhaps you are feeling a bit guilty. Relax. Take a deep breath. Keep on reading.

Throughout this book, I encourage us, as preservice and inservice teachers, to begin to write our own stories. Still, some of us just do not do so because we don't see the importance of such activity, or we feel we don't put words together well, or we don't have the time, or we're afraid of being judged and evaluated, or we think we don't spell well enough, or we think we don't know grammar well enough, or the pen hurts our hands and we get big callouses on our fingers, or, or, or ... There are really good reasons not to write. The avoidance of pain or vulnerability are good reasons to not write.

In this chapter, I discuss some of the reasons we choose to not write and offer some strategies for writing when we are reluctant to do so. For this chapter to work, you have got to be willing to take a risk. You might take the risk privately for a few minutes, or you might prefer to do it in a more social setting with trusted friends (see chap. 4 on support for writers). My friend Hanna is a writer, "a true friend and a good writer," and one whom I admire. One day, we were sitting together and there was a legal pad of yellow paper sitting between us. "That," she said, "is one of the scariest things there is."

"What is?" I asked.

"A blank sheet of paper."

She is right. When we are pressured to write, as for a required paper, some of us are terrified. Some of my graduate student friends and I were visiting one night and we began to brainstorm all the things we do to avoid starting our writing. We clean the house—especially toilets and other typically avoided areas—mow the lawn, run, jog, exercise, bake, take bubble baths, eat, use the phone, turn on the computer and clean it up (rather than begin writing). The list went on for about 10 minutes as we talked and laughed about avoidance strategies. Part of me began to wonder if perhaps these are not avoidance strategies as much as they are strategies for thinking.

ROADBLOCKS TO THINKING

Thinking is an important part of writing. Sadly, when I visit some elementary school classrooms, I see a chart of the five steps for writing—as if writing has some sort of linear sequence! The first step is usually brainstorming. Brainstorming is a powerful activity, but is rarely given the respect it deserves. Although I am sometimes helped by the strategy of thinking of, for example, as many things to write about as I can in 90 seconds, for me, brainstorming takes a lot longer and it doesn't necessarily involve generating long lists. I sort of "braindrizzle," with an occasional "brainburst" and downpour.

It's important to understand how you like to think and to respect that. If you know you get ideas when you sit in a bubble bath and eat chocolate chip cookies, then do that. You might want to keep a pad of paper and pencil handy so you can jot ideas down as they come to you. Don't let good ideas go down the drain!

That blinking cursor on a blank computer screen or that blank piece of paper evoke terror in the hearts and minds of some folks. Why? Some day watch a 2-year-old with some markers and paper. He or she will scribble and make cooing noises, sometimes so engrossed in writing that he or she forgets to swallow and begins to drool on the paper. Most of us never forget to swallow when confronted with blank paper as adults. In fact, our mouths go dry, our hands sweat, and the callous on the finger where the pencil rests hurts before that pencil even makes contact with the skin. It's fear.

We're afraid to fail.

We're afraid it won't be good enough for ... (Who? The teacher, the mother, the father, the lover ...)

We're afraid it is too short.

We're afraid there's a run-on sentence. Or a fragment.

We're afraid that it's awkward (and will be marked with some symbol that means such).

We're afraid of alphabet letters. (What if it gets a D or a C?)

We're afraid because someone somewhere along the line of our educational experience has told us that we are stupid. They might not have said it aloud and using that word, but they have said it. They said it with a red pen or a sad face or by not attaching a gold star when everyone else seemed to get one. Or they publicly embarrassed and humiliated us by posting a grade near our name, by making disapproving sounds while handing back papers, or by making us read in front of our peers when the reading would embarrass us.

In Irene Paull's (1972) touching and true story, a young child came home from school hysterical because she had wet her pants, having not been brave enough to tell the teacher that she needed to use the restroom. The very predictable reality unfolds:

> but I saw Mama looking down at me. Her eyes were sorrowful, but unrelenting. From what one must do there is no escape. Tomorrow I would have to go back to school. And nobody could help me ... [or] protect me from this fearful thing that every child must do. Nobody could know my suffering and nobody could share it with me. I was all alone in the world and tomorrow I would have to go ... far from my ghetto ... to die among strangers. (p. 10)

For many of us, school was a place where part of us had to die each day because death offered us numbness from what we felt was inflicted upon us, especially when it came to writing (though math runs a close second for many elementary school teachers).

Others of us were more lucky in that we didn't have to face such intensity of fear, but we died in another way. Slowly, because of the boredom, we simply stopped being the creative, playful youths we once were. Even John Dewey (1938) knew this:

> How many students ... were rendered callous to ideas, and how many lost the impetus to learn because of the way in which learning was experienced by them? How many acquired special skills by means of automatic drill so that their power of judgment and capacity to act intelligently in new situations was limited? How many came to associate the learning process with ennui and boredom? How many found what they did learn so foreign to the situations of life outside the school as to give them no power or control over the latter? (p. 27)

The factory-like atmosphere of many schools makes creativity an unwelcomed activity. Thus, we simply turned it off and the switch to turn it back on seems old and rusty now, when, in our later years, someone says that it's important to turn it back on. It is important because unless we do, we perpetuate the boredom or humiliation that so many students live out each day in school. Look back at Melissa's literacy autobiography for poignant evidence of death in the classroom.

OVERCOMING THE ROADBLOCKS

Why bother? Why overcome the many years of accumulated anxiety, fear, embarrassment, pain, or boredom? If all we want to do is teach, can't we just do it and not have the stuff of who we are in the way? Lucy Calkins (1994) offered some explanation. Early in her book, she said that "Writing does not begin with deskwork but with lifework" (p. 3). It would be so easy to say, 'of course that's true; but it is the children's lifework that I will nurture in my classroom and mine doesn't have to enter into it.' Calkins showed throughout the rest of the book that it is us—the self within us—that allows or disallows genuineness and authenticity in children's writing. She wrote:

> If we can begin to fathom how much our teaching matters, then perhaps we will begin to take more responsibility for nourishing ourselves as teachers and as people. In the end, what we bring to our classrooms is ourselves. Because our teaching matters so very much, we have a responsibility to take care of ourselves as learners and hopers and dreamers. (p. 517)

So when we take care of ourselves, let ourselves be learners, hopers, and dreamers, we are developing one of the most powerful teaching tools in our classrooms: ourselves.

Here, then, are some strategies for developing ourselves as writers of our stories, of our students' stories, and of the stories of the lives within and beyond school.

Time

Writing takes time. We have to give ourselves that time. Nancie Atwell (1987) teaches middle-school students in Maine. She taught me, through her writing, that writers need to give themselves the gift of time. Writers need time to think and daydream and play with ideas. We need time to imagine the beginning of our pieces, the development of them, and the ending. We need time because time is freedom. It is freedom to think, explore within our own minds, and hold our thinking against the various realities we see each day.

The time I spend thinking is time that I count when I tell someone how many hours I wrote on a given day. Putting pencil to paper, or fingertips to keyboard, is only one part of writing. Some days I spend time thinking of opening sentences (leads) to begin a piece. I read other writers' leads in articles, books, and newspapers. How do they start? Do I like it? Do I feel dramatic today, and want to start with: "The entire class stared at me in disbelief as I took off my belt, wiggled my hips and said, "Okay, it's time for science"? Or, do I want to start in a scholarly way with a thought from deep in my mind (or someone else's mind)?

Perhaps you want to go right to the middle, to the part that is so important that it wants to be written right away. You don't have to start your writing of a story at the beginning. You can write various parts and put them together quite literally with scissors and tape. Write what is in your heart and mind. Giving yourself the time to explore is a key point here. That is how you will learn to write. Annie Dillard (1989) responding to someone who asked her "Who will teach me to write?" wrote:

> The page, the page, that eternal blankness, the blankness of eternity which you cover slowly, affirming time's scrawl as a right and your daring as necessity; the page, which you cover suddenly, ruining it, but asserting your freedom and power to act, acknowledging that you ruin everything you touch but touching it nevertheless, because acting is better than being here in mere opacity; the page, which you cover slowly with the crabbed thread of your gut; the page in the purity of its possibilities; the page of your death, against which you pit such flawed excellences as you can muster with all your life's strength: that page will teach you to write. (pp. 58–59)

Let the page teach you to write. Sit with the page. Find yourself in it or through it. Write your life and you will see your life transform from a series of actions and activities to a complex tapestry woven of the many strands of your actions and activities. And the writing will bring sense to your life because writing is not merely recording your life, it is the time spent cultivating your thinking (Langer & Applebee, 1987).

Daydreaming

Carl Rogers (1956) wrote, "It seems to me that at bottom each person is asking: 'Who am I, *really?* How can I get in touch with the real self, underlying all my surface behavior? How can I become myself?'" (p. 197). As teachers, we are constantly struggling for identity. Our district tells us to use certain curricula (Goodman, Shannon, Freeman, & Murphy, 1987), yet our children are predisposed to study other things. Our principals or course instructors may be demanding in ways that don't make sense. The history of education (Shannon, 1990) points out that women, who comprise most of the elementary school teacher population, have been dominated and suppressed as teachers. There is a struggle for self in teaching. It is a struggle I urge teachers to pay attention to and to cultivate in themselves. It is a struggle that relies on dreaming of all the possibilities for ourselves and our students; a struggle to daydream our way into new possibilities. Alvina Burrows (1959) made an important connection between daydreaming and creative activity:

> How great is our bounty? An inheritance of millions! Not of dollars but of opportunities. Millions of children, millions of moments when their human need of communication quickens to life the sparks of creativity! For the future nothing is more important than these sparks, whether only aglow or already incandescent, should light the way to new freedom and new awareness. The test of education in a democracy may well be the degree to which individuals learn to trust their soul's invincible surmise and thus ... discover new continents, not of lands but of ideas and of ethics; new dreams by which to fashion themselves anew in music and dance and electricity; in clay and chemicals and wood; and in the enduring majesty of written words ... (p. 7)

My commitment to the importance of daydreaming comes from many frames. It comes from having read and studied with Carl Rogers. It comes from growing up near New York City in the way I described in chapter 1. It comes from a fascination with Zen Buddhism, and reading, and meditating, and deciding that I can create myself in many different ways.

I constantly daydream. I drive the *Starship Enterprise* and fire photon torpedoes at lousy drivers in the city in which I live. I'm a rock star in the acoustically delightful bathroom in which I shower. Sometimes, an odor will trigger a daydream, like the smell of an older-than-me man who smells like my dad. I daydream about my teaching, picturing myself in the classroom doing certain things, almost as a way of rehearsing what it is I want to do or hope will happen, and I daydream about my writing. I daydream about the audience (I talk more about audience later), about responses to my writing, and about myself as a scholar. I get into arguments with myself about a piece of writing before it's even written. That way, I write what I believe to be a stronger piece.

Why do it? Why daydream? Geane Hanson (1992) offers this:

> When researchers and teachers are willing to be self exposed, unifying their experience of mind and matter, the heart becomes more than a muscle. The heart becomes a metaphor for understanding, our way of seeing, feeling, interpreting and even creating the world in conjunction with our mind. Daydreaming becomes fascinating and contributes to the development of children's lives and authentic literacy processes. (p. 251)

Daydreaming is a vehicle, and expressing the stuff of our daydreams (through our writing, speaking, or dramatizing) is the conduit that leads us to become ourselves.

The following section is on oral language. John O. Stevens (1971) provided a good connection between oral language and daydreaming. By quoting him, I let him make the connection. He does it so well. I'll let him frame what comes next. He found that talking about (and writing about) a daydream

> deepens the feeling of identification with the fantasy experience and helps you realize that this is not "just a fantasy" but is an important expression of yourself and your life situation ...
>
> Another value in immediately telling someone else your fantasy is that you are communicating directly to another person. As you tell ... about your feelings and experiences ... you will often find that what you say is far more honest and personal than your usual way of speaking to others. You will often reveal quite a lot about yourself and your existence and you can experience how others respond to your honesty. It is valuable to become more aware of yourself, and it is also important to communicate your awareness to someone else so that your life is connected with others in honest contact. (pp. 137–138)

Oral Language

Talk about your life, the stories that make your family so unique, your experiences, and how you got to be you and not someone else. It's important that we value our oral stories—our oral traditions—because they tell us and others who we are. They set the stage for understanding oral traditions that develop in our classrooms.

One summer I worked as a teacher with the Upward Bound program in northern New York. The program provides academic and other types of support to Native American students nearing the completion of high school so that they can continue their education by attending college. The summer program offers academic skills, social activities, and the opportunity for the students to spend 6 weeks living on a college campus and taking classes. It provided me with many insights into a culture other than my own.

One cloudy day in the middle of summer, we loaded ourselves (2 teachers and 12 students) into a van and drove to the reservation to listen to a respected storyteller and author. Native American storytellers are an important part of their culture. Storytellers are valued for their multiple functions in that they deal with health, morality, ethics, history, aggression, culture, and so on. They can take the pulse of a culture and report back via the story they tell.

The storyteller told the tale of a young child who was impolite to his parents. The parents first spoke to the child about this, but he continued to be rude. Then one day, the father filled his mouth with water. When the child approached and was rude, the father blew the water into the child's face.

We were told that such a message from a father was usually a sufficient reminder to the child to be respectful of family members. This child continued to be disrespectful. The parents, deeply hurt, ignored the child. No place was set for the child at family meals and he was excluded from other events. When the child spoke, kindly or otherwise, they ignored him. They looked through their son as though he was not there.

I do not remember how long they did this. I don't remember how the story was resolved. I do remember the silence. Twelve students and two teachers sat; I felt that we were sitting within the story. As a stranger to the reservation culture, I said nothing and took my cues from the behavior of the students. The story seemed to be penetrating all of us. It began to rain.

After what seemed like an interminably long silence after the story, the storyteller asked the students to follow him outside so that he could show them around his land. The students followed him and I remember thinking that he never said, "And the moral of the story is ..." He knew how to tell a story that could teach without preaching. Storytelling is a delicate thing that changes from place to place and time to time, but it always teaches. It is different in different cultures, but it has a common thread in that it, as Gregory Clark (1990) said, helps to "create a common conception of reality" (p. 36). Our stories bind, mix, shape, alienate, remind, link, change, and impact us. Their oral telling is powerful and important and it teaches the teller as well as the listeners.

Telling our stories aloud is one way of contributing them to the collection of stories that are the substantive form of who we are as teachers and learners. We often sit in class, or informally at one of our homes, and answer stories with stories for hours. We make sense of our teaching and learning through our stories. Dave Wilson and Joy Ritchie (1994) referred to teachers' stories as *narratives* and justified their use this way:

> These stories become a kind of primary text in [our] classes, enabling us to uncover our unspoken assumptions; examine the contradictions between our pedagogies and our experiences; complicate our understandings of literacy, learning, and teaching; integrate our examined experiences into our working conceptions of literacy and learning; develop intimacy and build community. They also provide us with a sense of our own authority to resist and revise the powerful culture of schools. (p. 85)

There's a powerful idea here: Stories 'complicate our understandings,' rather than simplify and reduce them. Our stories reveal, support, lead to understanding, and create the oral tradition of who we are and how we go about our lives.

When a story becomes a tape-in-my-mind that I can play over and over, I know it is time to examine it more closely because it has become rote; it is losing its intrapersonal importance. My story is partly performance, but it is also a vehicle for my learning. When the story becomes a tape, it runs with what seems to be an automaticity that may be useful to the listener who has never heard it before, but it is not that useful for me. I work at making a story an intrapersonal (within me) as well as interpersonal (between myself and others) experience. I try to make it meaningful to myself and to those to whom I am telling it.

Oral traditions are part of our backgrounds. Our families have stories and share these stories as a way of bonding, passing along family history, and perpetuating values and ideas. Our classrooms have stories that become part of the oral traditions of our classrooms through the stories of our lives together. In a second-grade classroom, part of the oral tradition may be the recounting of the time that the children in the baking center put in one cup of salt instead of one teaspoon of salt when they were baking some peanut butter cookies. The resulting feast-turned-to-a-dash-for-the-water-fountain becomes part of the collective of stories that make the classroom specific and unique.

In one undergraduate course I taught, we reminisced about favorite teachers and what made them so special to us. We were sharing our recollections and understanding of the classroom cultures each of those teachers nurtured. I went home and wrote in my journal:

> Does an undergraduate class have a culture that we share? Are they so worried about grades and course requirements that they just don't want to or can't develop a culture that goes beyond 'how do we play school here? How do I get my grade and get out?'
>
> What can I do to own this idea? What is my responsibility as far as supporting them and me in getting rid of some of that baggage about what school should be like?

During the next class session, I found myself at the front of the room doing something that sounds bizarre. I was asking the class how many synonyms they could think of for *tush* (i.e., buttocks). The list was long and we laughed a lot. The reason for the 'tush discussion,' as it came to be called, was that earlier in the class session, I was standing at the front of the classroom and began writing on the board. I noticed something that, in all my years of teaching, I had not noticed before. As I wrote on the board, I could feel my tush wiggle. I suppose that over the years it had lost some of its muscle tone.

I cannot recall what I was writing, but instantly I remembered my fourth-grade teacher. The movement of my own body—a kinesthetic activity—triggered a recollection. Mrs. C was warm and caring and very overweight. One day, when she was writing on the board, I noticed that each stroke of her arm had a sort of opposite reaction along her tush. The more furiously she wrote on the board, the more her tush wiggled. I didn't laugh or make fun; I was more intrigued by the ripples that crossed this massive body area.

I turned to the undergraduates and told them what I was thinking, about my own body becoming sort of flabby and my recollection of Mrs. C. It was as though I had broken some rule that had never been stated: Never admit that you are watching a teacher's tush when he or she is writing on the board. The laughter became uncontrollable as it filled the room. We were quite out of control. I said, "Okay, now wait. I called it a 'tush,' but what are the other names for it? I think that this is a part of our bodies that has more different names than any other body part." The brainstorming began. And periodically, throughout the semester, someone would raise their hand and announce that they had heard or remembered another name for that part.

The tush event, in that undergraduate class, was an important moment in my college teaching career because it helped me realize that a community of learners is a possibility with undergraduates. We needed, as part of being a community, stories that were uniquely ours. Sharing our literacy autobiographies does this; so do unplanned events that we cultivate and enculture as parts of our shared lived experiences.

We have those lived events—shared experiences— as memories. The next challenge, then, is taking the leap from oral to written form. If you were to audiotape your story as you told it and then transcribe that tape, you would probably not like what you heard. There are subtle differences between oral and written language—the exact same words in oral form are different when written. So, typically, transcribing a story doesn't work. I find it useful to picture myself telling the story to a group or individual; but once I start writing, the pencil takes charge and forms the story differently than my mouth would form it. This isn't so hard to understand when we take a common example. Suppose you are about to leave your home to go shopping for some shoes. If someone with whom you live is at home and you want them to know where you are going, you might say, "I'm going to get some shoes. See you later." But if no one is home and you want to leave a note to let folks know where you are, you might write:

Sue—
I'm going to get some shoes. See you later.
Rick

Aren't those the same? Well, they might be the same in meaning. In the writing you provided more information so that the reader knows the same things the listener would know in the earlier situation. In an oral interchange, you don't have to say the person's name and you don't have to say who the message is from if it's from you. A lot is understood because you and the listener are physically present. In story writing, the subtleties of physical presence are gone and you, the writer, provide more information so the reader can understand what you mean.

It's important to know about these subtleties because getting good at oral storytelling is a powerful part of being a teacher and learner. It also predisposes you to story writing. However, the jump from oracy to writing is not necessarily easy. So, if you are telling stories orally and then decide to write and are experiencing some discomfort, that's okay! It is to be expected.

I think discomfort is part of the tension that writers feel. The discomfort and tension are part of being creative because creativity requires energy; tension and discomfort (as well as other emotional or cognitive states) put stress on our lives and we can learn to use that stress to push ourselves as writers. We live our lives, feel the tension, live the story as it unfolds, tell the story in order to relive and enhance it, and eventually write the story. This can be a long, slow process, one that allows us to understand all the many facets of the story, the players involved, and the context in which it all takes place.

Summing up this section on oral language would go like this: Live your life, tell your life, know that telling your life changes your life, write your life, know that writing your life changes your life. Live with others, tell your life with others, know that telling your life with others changes your life and theirs, write your life with others, know that writing your life with others changes your life and theirs. It enriches, deepens understanding, clarifies, elaborates, questions, focuses, intensifies, and complicates.

Needless to say, trust is a key issue in storytelling. We need a caring, safe community in which to tell our stories. We might also want a community that inspires us to write the story down because our writing of it will change it, will change us, and will change others.

> Current theory in oral conversation is founded upon the fundamental recognition ... that people engage in conversation for the purpose of coordinating their separate interpretations of experience to establish shared meanings ... not only does [conversation] function socially to create the common conception of reality upon which cooperation can be based, but the very process of sustaining it requires members of a community to participate in an exchange in which those connections are continuously revised and extended. (Clark, 1990, pp. 36–37)

So ... talk.

Reading

Reading helps our writing. Reading shows us how others write. Reading is an ongoing demonstration of some of the possible ways of writing. We study a writer's style as we read what that writer has written. We might look at the length of the piece, its style, its voice, the use of big words, and other salient features of the writing. As we read, we learn how to write (and as we write, we learn how to read). Reading the same book or article as our colleagues may lead to discussions about the content or about the way the author wrote. Both types of discussion may help us as writers.

We might want to respond in anger or agreement or some other way to something someone has written. You can do that in writing. Sometimes I invite a class to read letters written to various columnists in the newspaper (like *Dear Abby*) and we write our responses and compare our writing to the columnists'. We also write responses to articles and books that we read. Writing responses is a very legitimate form of writing. It leads to interactive journals, which I view as continuous response-writing. We can do this on paper or using electronic mail on our computers. These are all ways to express our voices in writing.

Dramatizing

I first met Ericka when she was a student in a graduate course I was teaching. Part of the possible course requirements (each student actually designed a personalized course) was the writing of a literacy autobiography. Ericka asked, "Could I dance mine? My literacy autobiography is about me and I'm so hyper and probably would be labeled if I was in school today ... couldn't I just dance it?" She was only half serious because she wanted to rediscover her literacy. She had read Don Graves (1990) and wanted to retrace the steps of her literacy life for the many reasons he described in that book.

Ericka is a dancer. She works at the district office as the early childhood consultant in our city, but every teacher of young children in the district knows her as a dancer. She radiates warmth, caring, and energy. She is constantly moving, thinking, indeed, dancing with the issues she confronts each day on the job. She could have danced her literacy autobiography. And she would have wanted us all to dance along, as well.

Ericka made me realize that not all of us want to discover self-expression via written activity. We are painters, sculptors, potters, singers, musicians, mathematicians, meditators, and more. Clearly, for most of us in our society, written language is the expectation. Art, dance, and music may carry prestige, but writing carries prestige and expectation. It is expected that we will be writers in some facet of our lives. But we do not have to start there. We can begin our journey into our literacy lives, and the lives of the children we teach, by respecting and cultivating other ways of expressing selfness. These other modes of expression are windows into ourselves. They can teach us who we are and that knowledge will transform our understanding of our classrooms.

This section could have been entitled play with clay, or paint your life, or create a photo montage, or talk while you bake, or finger-paint today, or walk the beaches, and so on. Any of these activities or projects relaxes us and puts us in the state of mind to let our thoughts and language flow. Think aloud as you play and you are on your way to writing. And when you do begin, start from what is real for you. Start as small or as big as you like. Start with a list, a note, a letter, an article, or a novel. Start with a poem or a word.

WRITING

Writers and other artists are often portrayed as troubled souls who deal with pain through the pen. Natalie Goldberg (1986) wrote:

> To begin writing from our pain eventually engenders compassion for our small and groping lives. Out of this broken state there comes a tenderness for the cement below our feet, the dried grass cracking in a terrible wind. We can touch the things around us we once thought ugly and see their special detail, the peeling paint and gray of shadows as they are—simply what they are; not bad, just part of the life around us—and love this life because it is ours and in the moment there is nothing better. (p. 107)

Writing from pain is at once easy and painful. It is easy when pain is real and pervasive to the self and so present and so real that it's the only thing that truly makes sense as a topic of our writing. That reality and persuasiveness also make writing difficult because of what we must do to write it, to commit it to paper. We must know it and shape it onto paper. There is that omnipresent (and necessary) tension when we write. My past struggles with itself, my present, and the future. My 'used to be' struggles with my 'want to be.' My hopes and dreams struggle with my perceived reality.

But our writing does not always have to emanate from pain. Our love, lust, joy, exhilaration, temptations, fears, wondering, curiosity, and the entire breadth of our emotional lives are the raw materials for our writing lives. Our experiences and all of the emotional baggage those experiences carry are important. They matter. They are worth writing about. It is essential that we have a carefully selected community of writers with whom to share our writing because presentation and exploration of our writing is presentation and exploration of ourselves. This is about relationships and it is an intimate activity.

As a teacher, you are unique in that your job consists of supporting writers. Mem Fox (1993) argued:

> that if we are so foolish as to dare to teach writing without ever writing ourselves, we are trading with arrogance on shaky ground. … Unless we experience *firsthand* the agonies and ecstasies of writing, we may fast discredit this new method of engaging in inept and inappropriate classroom practice. (pp. 35–36)

We write so that our students' writing may be authentic and genuine; we create a place in which writers feel the tension of the work that they do and can explore and use that tension to compose themselves as writers.

The Writer's Setting

A few years ago, at a local conference of the International Reading Association, I attended a presentation by Patricia Riely Giff, the children's author. She said that she has a separate space that she rents for her writing. She goes there each day, turns on her computer, and then wraps herself in the shawl that her grandmother gave her. She lies on the floor and pictures characters from her books. She imagines what might be in their pockets. When you read her books, you don't know what's in characters' pockets, but that's how those characters were created. They were created in a special-to-the-author place as she lay wrapped in a piece of her own story. I could see her, walking to that place, wrapping herself, the light coming in through a window (that she did not mention in her telling), and I also saw a braided rug on that floor. That was her writing place, the setting for her work.

I wanted a special place to write. I wanted it to be like the writer's womb that Madeline Grumet (1992) described. When she writes, she sits at the computer in her office surrounded by books she loves. She hasn't read some of them, but she loves that they are there, with her, in her writer's setting. She refers to it as a womb for her thinking and writing. She says that above Kafka's writing table that famous author had a single word attached to the wall: Wait. So, as writers, sometimes we go to that writing setting and we wait.

I didn't feel as lucky as Patricia and Madeline. Where I live now, the basement is my study and there are no windows. My office is cinderblock and has a view of a window when the door is open and I lean out a bit. But there is no view. Still, I seem to get a lot of writing done in both places. Annie Dillard (1989) helped me live easier with my situation:

> Appealing workplaces are to be avoided. One wants a room with no view, so imagination can meet memory in the dark. When I furnished this study seven years ago, I pushed the long desk against a blank wall, so I could not see from either window. Once, fifteen years ago, I wrote in a cinder-block cell over a parking lot. It overlooked a tar-and-gravel roof. This pine shed under trees is not quite so good as the cinder-block study was, but it will do.

> "The beginning of wisdom," according to a West African proverb, "is to get you a roof." (pp. 26–27)

Well, I 'got me a roof,' but would I write better if I had a window?

Once again, the important thing here is self. What is it you need as a setting for your writing? Do you need many different kinds of pens, certain paper, a computer, lucky socks, lots of chocolate? Which of these truly help? Do you like to write for 10 minutes a day or 10 hours a day. Are you a marathon writer or a sprinter? Is the radio on loud or do you need silence? All of these are important considerations for a writer and, as should be obvious because so many of them seem to be at opposite ends of some kind of writing spectrum, all of them are quite impossible to accommodate in a classroom of 25 children. That may be why you came out of school as a nonwriter or an antiwriter—because you needed something that the setting lacked.

There are a variety of possibilities for you to explore, then. You may want to spend time building a beautiful safe womb-like space for your writing activity. Or, you may want a setting that is more like a writing bunker that keeps everything out so that you can get into your mind. Learning about yourself as a writer involves knowing the difference between creating a space in which you can write and avoidance of writing by spending extensive periods of time changing that space. It means knowing the difference between cleaning the house because it is dirty or because it helps you think in your own very personal kind of 'brainweather' (be it brainstorms, drizzles, flurries, or anything in between).

Create a setting that supports you in your writing.

Then, write.

Afterward, you will be able to approach your classroom as a writer and cocreate, with the writers there, a space in which writers can flourish.

The Writer's Tools

I've mentioned some of the tools of the writing craft throughout various parts of this book. Choose tools you are comfortable with and ones that don't tax your writing hand (or hands if you use a keyboard). There is something quite romantic about a legal pad of yellow paper and a No. 2 pencil. I like to write and erase and cross out. I like the sounds that pencils make. Shop around for the tools you prefer.

Once I entered graduate school full time, I needed a computer. I now type faster than I can write, so using a keyboard is often my tool of choice. Also, sometimes I close my eyes and type. This relaxes my eyes and lets me get deeper into my mind. There have been times, though, where I come too close to falling asleep when I type this way; also, I have to make sure my fingers are in the right position on the keyboard to avoid getting letter strings (but no words) on the page. I still do revising in pencil on hard copies. I like the idea of moving from the computer chair to another seat in the house or office; this makes writing less physically intense.

Suggested Books on Writing.   I suppose that for some of us it's a lot easier to read about writing than to actually write. Others may want to read more to gather a broader repertoire of strategies for approaching the blank page or computer screen. Some important books on writing are listed at the end of this chapter. I do not intend this to be a comprehensive list, but it is a beginning, and includes my favorites.

Audience

When I get stuck, frightened, overwhelmed, paralyzed, or frozen about my writing, I think of who I want to write a piece for. It's as though the entire book or article becomes a letter to someone who is a safe, caring audience.

Fantasize about who will read your story. Get their picture in your head, let your words and frames melt together, and let the story unfold to a good friend, to your good listener, to the person who lets you spend time exploring your thoughts and your dreams. This is the person to write to because he or she is the one who will let you be yourself and say things the way you like. Picture that person. With all of his or her patience and caring, let that person be there for you as you write.

If you don't have someone like that, invent him or her. Take a face you like, one you see as you walk or drive or travel around where you live or even see in a movie or on television, and attach to that face all the attributes you want in a good-for-you audience. They laugh in the right places, their eyes glow and become teary when they should, and they tell you what you need to hear: Your writing is okay. Even if you know you will revise many times, let this person be the one who sees through the superficiality of the words. This is the person who sees the potential in the piece of writing, and in you, and celebrates both with you. Even though he or she is a fantasy, he or she will do until you find an audience with which you feel safe in taking the risk of presenting your writing.

My friend Hanna is a very important (and real) support person for me. When I was stuck in a black hole of doom about my writing, she sent me *The Writing Life* by Annie Dillard (1989) and, on the inside cover, she wrote, "So you know you're not alone." She reminded me that she is there as a cowriter. She struggles with her writing and I struggle with mine. She knows the life of a writer better than I do because she's been at it longer and studied herself harder. I am rich to have her. Our relationship took many years to develop and we both know that.

Some writers' audience is less terrestrial and more spiritual. Such an audience is loving and supportive. For other writers, other groups or individuals work as a safe audience. The crucial point is that you give yourself time to find that audience you need, especially for those first few pieces.

Agenda

In chapter 3, on longer stories, I wrote about my daughter, Zoe. She has an agenda for her written language activity. She writes with intensity and motivation that come from a deep place. When I watch her, I can see a story percolate up from her heart and mind as she writes with passion and commitment. We need to write about things that are important to us. We spend so much time writing for others' agendas: instructors, the government, a boss, a principal, a committee, and so on. When do we write what lives within? When do we 'write down the bones'?

Now.

Write now. Write from the heart. Write in metaphors or in blunt text. Write on graph paper or on the outside of envelopes as you ride the train. Write the story of you so that you can support the writers in your classroom as they write their stories.

A writer's agenda is rooted in the writer's choice; this is referred to as *ownership*. When you write from your agenda, you own the piece of writing. It is yours. You may choose to share it, change it, dump it, or hide it away in a secret place, but it is yours. You make all the major decisions about the piece.

Surprise

Surprise is an element of writing that makes it a process of discovery, uncovering, revelation, and fun. An author might or might not know that the story he or she writes is going to have a surprise. Don Murray (1985) said that "surprise is the most significant element in writing. It is the motivating force that makes writers of us and of our students" (pp. 180–181). We might be surprised as we collect our story, as we search for evidence. Sometimes we surprise ourselves in our writing, as we write and find that memories are flooding back and changing, or that things are falling into place in ways we didn't expect. This is what writing does; it changes our thinking (Langer & Applebee, 1987), our histories, our present, and our future.

I usually keep a journal when I teach a class. Writing about the class, as close as possible to the end of each day helps me to understand my role, the roles of the students, the dynamics between and among us, and so on. One evening, teaching a graduate course, I looked up and saw my reflection in the windows of the classroom. Later that night, I wrote a journal entry, part of which follows.

When I am teaching, I have more hair. This evening we were having quite a lively discussion . .... Folks had read a lot and were anxious to respond to the reading in light of their own teaching experiences. We were quite immersed in conversation when suddenly the darkness of the outside caught my attention. I realized that while we were having class, the sun had set and the city had become quite dark. This was only a brief moment, I don't usually "leave" a class when I am teaching. As my visual attention was refocusing into the classroom, that thin layer of glass separating us from the night elements reflected someone vaguely familiar, but surely it could not be me.

Yet, it was. My mouth began to move as I rejoined the conversation and I was, once again, drawn into the discussion. Driving home after class, the image of that person in the glass came back into my head. That's not me, I thought. That couldn't be me. The person in the glass was, well, he was pretty bald on top. I rubbed the top of my head. When did this happen, I found myself wondering. When did I become old looking? Why didn't I feel like I was old until I looked at myself? I knew I was losing hair ... well, and some hearing, too. And I find myself doing what I saw my parents doing, something which always seemed like such a waste of time: I take naps with the newspaper on Sundays.

But teaching does something. When I am with a class and they are excited about the context, engaged and present, I feel young and energized. I feel like I have a full head of bushy curly hair. I feel fresh and refreshed. Classroom activity seems to enliven and rejuvenate me.

There was something about the lighting, the dark of the city in contrast with the light of the classroom, and seeing myself in the contrasting light that made me realize I am past middle age, I'm mortal, and I'm temporary.

That 'seeing' of myself would have been forgotten, except that I wrote it down. And as I wrote, I realized that I was old, or older than I picture myself. The glimpse of myself was an instant in time, but the writing brought the surprise of "me" and a depth of understanding about my aging and mortality.

IT'S TIME ...

Writing is a courageous act. Rollo May (1975) wrote, "Every profession can and does require some creative courage" (p. 15). As teachers, telling the stories of our teaching and learning lives and the lives of the children in our classrooms, we need to be courageous. Our writing is the way we truly link ourselves with our work, with our students, and with our colleagues in the small community of a writers' group or the larger community of writers who publish in more traditional ways. Our writing is a window into our souls, our 'selfs'—it is one of the most powerful and growthful things we can do and it takes courage. Although we risk our very sensitive lives with each scratch of a pencil, I know that it is time to write. It is time to connect with ourselves and our students and let our voices be heard. Writing brings meaning to our lives in a way that is unique to writing—so find your own uniqueness: Write.

I began this chapter with a quote from *Charlotte's Web* (White, 1952). Charlotte's life as a writer changed her and changed those around her. Her writing was important. She knew that; the other members of the barn community knew that.

She knew that by writing, she was actively being part of the story that is created as lives wrap themselves around each other.

When Charlotte was dying, she knew that her work as a writer had changed Wilbur's world, the way our writing may change our lives and the lives of the children with whom we work. In what turned out to be her last conversation with her friend, Wilbur, Charlotte tried to make sense of life, just as we writers seek to make sense of life:

> A moment later a tear came to Wilbur's eye. "Oh, Charlotte," he said. "To think that when I first met you I thought you were cruel and bloodthirsty!"
>
> When he recovered from his emotion, he spoke again.
>
> "Why did you do all this for me?" he asked. "I don't deserve it. I've never done anything for you."
>
> "You have been my friend," replied Charlotte. "That in itself is a tremendous thing. I wove my webs for you because I liked you. After all, what's a life, anyway? We're born, we live a little while, we die. A spider's life can't help being something of a mess, with all this trapping and eating flies. By helping you, perhaps I was trying to lift up my life a trifle. Heaven knows anyone's life can stand a little of that." (p. 164)

POSTSCRIPT

Still not writing?

Even though you believe that our lives can be 'something of a mess' and could use a little lifting up, are you still out of touch with the writer within you?

Lenny Kleinfold is a writer, humorist, and commentator on National Public Radio. On July 13, 1994, as I was driving home from the office where I was outlining this book, he was talking about writer's block. He said that when writers can't write, they usually do one of a few things. One is to "resort to cheap sex," another is alcohol, and the third is to go into therapy. "None of these work," he added.

Lenny needed to pick up his wife at the airport. Still feeling quite blocked, he decided to shave off his beard before picking her up. He felt that his wife, seeing him without his beard (which he had worn for many years), would provide the inspiration he needed, if he was not inspired before then. When he met his wife, he was flooded with inspiration. Lenny had nudged his life just a bit, just enough to make things slightly different. For some of us, that's all we need. Change the patterns of our existence a bit and part of us, deep within, seems rattled. That rattling produces a chain reaction. Writers pay attention to those rattles within their lives. When there isn't enough rattling going on, they instigate it a bit by doing things like shaving, dying their hair, walking a different route home, changing their views of the world ever so slightly (tilting their heads sideways, looking down instead of up, or doing things in a new or different order for a day or two).

Writers also know that the natural movement of the world may be enough to inspire them to write. The act of writing is an act of focusing on that movement. Your world is always moving and your writing is a way of making sense of (or making fun of, or celebrating, or expressing sorrow over) your world. This is especially true of us, as teachers and learners. Our writing is our mechanism for making sense of the many worlds in which we—with our students, colleagues, and community—live.

SUGGESTED READING

Dillard, A. (1989). *The writing life.* New York: HarperCollins.

Elbow, P. (1981). *Writing with power: Techniques for mastering the writing process.* New York: Oxford University Press.

Fletcher, F. (1993). *What a writer needs.* Portsmouth, NH: Heinemann.

Fox, M. (1993). *Radical reflections: Passionate opinions on teaching, learning, and living.* San Diego, CA: Harcourt Brace.

Goldberg, N. (1986). *Writing down the bones: Freeing the writer within.* Boston: Shambhala.

Murray, D. (1984). *Write to learn.* New York : Holt, Rinehart & Winston.

Paterson, K. (1981). *Gates of excellence: On reading and writing books for children.* New York: Dutton.

References

Applebee, A. N. (1984). Writing and reasoning. *Review of Educational Research, 54*(4), 577–596.

Ashton-Warner, S. (1971). *Teacher.* New York: Bantam.

Atwell, N. (1987). *In the middle: Writing, reading, and learning with adolescents.* Portsmouth, NH: Heineman.

Au, K. (1981). Participation structures in a reading lesson with Hawaiian children: Analysis of a culturally appropriate instructional event. *Anthropology and Education Quarterly, XI*(2), 91–115.

Birdseye, T. (1993). *Just call me stupid.* New York: Holliday House.

Bissex, G. (1980). *GNYS AT WRK: A child learns to read and write.* Cambridge, MA: Harvard University Press.

Burrows, A. (1959, February). Children's written composition: Introduction. *Elementary English.*

Bloome, D. (1983). Reading as a social process. *Advances in Reading/Language Research, 2,* 165–195.

Calkins, L. (1983). *Lessons from a child: On the teaching and learning of writing.* Portsmouth, NH: Heineman.

Calkins, L. (1986). *The art of teaching writing.* Portsmouth, NH: Heineman.

Calkins, L. (1994). *The art of teaching writing* (rev. ed.). Portsmouth, NH: Heineman.

Calkins, L. (1991). *Living between the lines.* Portsmouth, NH: Heineman.

Carini, P. (1979). *The art of seeing and the visibility of the person.* Grand Forks: University of North Dakota.

Carini, P. (1982). *The school lives of seven children: A five year study.* Grand Forks: University of North Dakota.

Carter, K. (1993). The place of story in the study of teaching and teacher education. *Educational Researcher, 22*(1), 5–12.

Cazden, C. (1988). *Classroom discourse: The language of teaching and learning.* Portsmouth, NH: Heineman.

Clark, G. (1990). *Dialogue, dialectic, and conversation: A social perspective on the function of writing.* Carbondale, IL: Southern Illinois University Press.

Clay, M. (1984). *What did I write: Beginning writing behavior.* Portsmouth, NH: Heineman.

Clay, M. (1987). *Writing begins at home: Preparing children for writing before they go to school.* Portsmouth, NH: Heineman.

Cochran-Smith, M., & Lytle, S. (1990). Research on teaching and teacher research: The issues that divide. *Educational Researcher, 19*(2), 2–11.

Cochran-Smith, M., & Lytle, S. (1993). *Inside outside: Teacher research and knowledge.* New York: Teachers' College Press.

Cochrane, O., & Buchanan, E. (Eds.). (1993). *Teacher stories: Starting the year with whole language.* Winnipeg: Whole Language Consultants.

Crowell, C. (1993). Living through war vicariously with literature. In L. Patterson, C. Santa, K. Short, & K. Smith (Eds.), *Teachers are researchers: Reflection and action* (pp. 51–59). Newark, DE: IRA.

Dahl, R. (1964). *Charlie and the chocolate factory.* New York: Knopf.

Dewey, J. (1904). The relation of theory to practice in education. In C. McMurry (Ed.), *The third yearbook of the National Society for the Scientific Study of Education* (pp. 9–30). Chicago: University of Chicago Press.

Dewey, J. (1938). *Experience and education.* New York: Collier Books/Macmillan.

Dewey, J. (1939). *Logic: The theory of inquiry.* New York: Holt, Rinehart & Winston.

Dillard, A. (1989). *The writing life.* New York: HarperCollins.

Dyson, A. H. (1993). *Social worlds of children learning to write in an urban primary school.* New York: Teachers' College Press.

Eastman, P. D. (1960). *Are you my mother?* New York: Random House.

Edelsky, C., & Smith, K. (1984). Is that writing—or are those marks just a figment of your curriculum? *Language Arts, 61*(1), 24–32.

Emig, J. (1971). *The composing processes of twelfth graders* (Rep. No. NCTE–RR–13). Urbana, IL: National Council of Tecahers of English. (ERIC Document Reproduction Service No. Ed 058 205)

Fox, M. (1993). *Radical reflections: Passionate opinions on teaching, learning, and living.* San Diego: Harcourt Brace.

Gentry, J. R. (1987). *Spel ... is a four-letter word.* Portsmouth, NH: Heineman.

Giacobbe, M. E. (1986). Learning to write and writing to learn in the elementary school. In A. Petrosky & D. Bartholomae (Eds.), *The teaching of writing: Eighty-fifty yearbook of the National Society for the Study of Education* (pp. 131–147). Chicago: University of Chicago Press.

Goldberg, N. (1986). *Writing down the bones: Freeing the writer within.* Boston: Shambala.

Goodman, K. (1986). *What's whole in whole language?* Portsmouth, NH: Heineman.

Goodman, K., Shannon, P., Freeman, Y., & Murphy, S. (1987). *Report card on the basal readers.* Katonah, NY: Richard C. Owens.

Goodman, Y. (1985). Kidwatching: Observing children in the classroom. In A. Jaggar & M. T. Smith-Burke (Eds.), *Observing the language learner* (pp. 9–18). Newark, DE: NCTE, IRA.

Graves, D. (1983). *Writing: Teachers and children at work.* Portsmouth, NH: Heineman.

Graves, D. (1990). *The reading/writing teacher's companion: Discover your own literacy.* Portsmouth, NH: Heineman.

Gray, M., & Troy, A. (1986). Elementary teachers of reading as models. *Reading Horizons, 31,* 179–184.

Grumet, M. (1991). The politics of personal knowledge. In P. Witherell & N. Noddings (Eds.), *Stories lives tell: Narrative and dialogue in education* (pp. 67–77). New York: Teachers' College Press.

Grumet, M. (1992, April). *Why read books with other people?* Paper presented at the annual meeting of the American Educational Research Association, San Francisco, CA.

Halliday, M. A. K. (1975). *Learning how to mean: Explorations in the development of language.* London: Edward Arnold.

Halliday, M. A. K. (1977). *Explorations in the functions of language.* New York: Elsevier.

Halliday, M. A. K. (1978). *Language as social semiotic: The social interpretation of language and meaning.* Baltimore: University Park Press.

Halliday, M. A. K. (1988). 'There's still a long way to go ...' An interview with emeritus professor Michael Halliday. *Journal of the Australian Advisory Council on Languages and Multicultural Education, 1,* 35—39.

Halliday, M. A. K., & Hasan, R. (1985). *Language, context, and text: Aspects of language in a social-semiotic perspective.* Victoria: Deakin University Press.

Hansen, J. (1987). *When writers read.* Portsmouth, NH: Heineman.

Harste, J., & Short, K., with Burke, C. (1988). *Creating classrooms for authors: The reading–writing connection.* Portsmouth, NH: Heineman.

Hanson, G. (1992). *My thinking chair: Daydreaming in the lives of children.* Unpublished doctoral dissertation, University of Arizona, Tucson.

Harste, J., Woodward, V., & Burke, C. (1984). *Language stories & literacy lessons.* Portsmouth, NH: Heineman.

Harwayne, S. (1992). *Lasting impressions: Weaving literature into the writing workshop.* Portsmouth, NH: Heineman.

Heath, S. B. (1983). *Ways with words: Language, life, and work in communities and classrooms.* Cambridge: Cambridge University Press.

Heilbrun, C. (1988). *Writing a woman's life.* New York: Norton.

Hill, M. (1989). *Home where writing and reading begin.* Portsmouth, NH: Heineman.

Hogan, L. (1987). The two lives. In B. Swarm & A. Arupat (Eds.), *I tell you now: Autobiographical essays by Native American writers* (pp. 231–250). Lincoln: University of Nebraska Press.

Hope, S. (1972). Relations stop nowhere. In M. Greer & B. Rubinstein (Eds.), *Will the real teacher please stand up?* (p. 110). Pacific Palisades, CA: Goodyear.

Houle, C. (1961). *The inquiring mind.* Madison: University of Wisconsin Press.

Hubbard, R. (1989). Notes from the underground: Unofficial literacy in one sixth grade. *Anthropology and Education Quarterly, 20*(4), 291–307.

Hubbard, R. S., & Power, B. M. (1993). *The art of classroom inquiry: A handbook for teacher researchers.* Portsmouth, NH: Heineman.

Hughes, L. (1967). *Don't you turn back: Poems by Langston Hughes.* New York: Knopf.

Klassen, C., & Short, K. (1992). Collaborative research on teacher study groups: Embracing the complexities. In C. Kinzer & D. Leu (Eds.), *Literacy research, theory, and practice: View from many perspectives, Forty first yearbook of the National Reading Conference* (pp. 341–348). Chicago: National Reading Conference.

Kohl, H. (1967). *36 children.* New York: Signet.

Kohl, H. (1991). *The role of assent in learning: I won't learn from you.* Minneapolis, MN: Milkweed.

Langer, J., & Applebee, A. (1987). *How writing shapes thinking: A study of teaching and learning.* Urbana, IL: NCTE.

Lareau, A. (1989). *Home advantage: Social class and parental intervention in elementary education.* London: The Falmer Press.

Manna, A., & Misherr, S. (1987). What teachers say about their own reading development. *Journal of Reading, 31,* 160–168.

May, R. (1975). *The courage to create.* New York: Bantam.

Mehan, H. (1982). The structure of classroom events and their consequences for student performance. In P. Gilmore & A. Glatthorn (Eds.), *Children in and out of school: Ethnography and education* (pp. 59–87). Washington, DC: Center for Applied Linguistics.

Meltzoff, N. (1993, October). *Ten fundamental strands in the development of a classroom community.* Paper presented at the Reconceptualizing Early Childhood Education Conference, Ann Arbor, MI.

Moll, L., & Diaz, S. (1987). Change as the goal of educational research. *Anthropology and Education Quarterly, 18*(4), 300–311.

Mour, S. (1977). Do teachers read? *The Reading Teacher, 30,* 397–401.

Murray, D. (1985). Writing and teaching for surprise. *Highway One, 8*(1–2), 174–181.

Neil, A. S. (1960). *Summerhill: A Radical approach to child rearing.* New York: Hart.

Newkirk, T. (1989). *More than stories: The range of children's writing.* Portsmouth, NH: Heineman.

Newman, D., Griffin, P., & Cole, M. (1989). *The construction zone: Working for cognitive change in school.* New York: Cambridge University Press.

Newman, J. (1991). *Interwoven conversations: Learning and teaching through critical reflection.* Toronto: OISE Press.

Paley, V. (1981). *Wally's stories: Conversations in the kindergarten.* Cambridge, MA: Harvard University Press.

Paley, V. (1990). *The boy who would be a helicopter: The uses of storytelling in the classroom.* Cambridge, MA: Harvard University Press.

Patterson, L., Santa, C. M., Short, K. G., & Smith, K. (Eds.). (1993). *Teachers are researchers: Reflection and action.* Newark, DE: International Reading Association.

Paull, I. (1972). To die among strangers. In M. Greer & B. Rubinstein (Eds.), *Will the real teacher please stand up?: A primer in humanistic education* (pp. 6–11). Pacific Palisades, CA: Goodyear.

Perrone, V. (1991). *A letter to teachers: Reflections on schooling and the art of teaching.* San Francisco: Jossey-Bass.

Philips, S. (1971). Participant structures and communicative competence: Warm Springs children in community and classroom. In C. Cazden, V. John, & D. Hymes (Eds.), *Functions of language in the classroom* (pp. 370–393). New York: Teachers College Press.

Polakow, V. (1993). *Lives on the edge: Single mothers and their children in the other America.* Chicago: University of Chicago Press.

Redford, R., & Markey, P. (Producers), & Redford, R. (Director). (1992). *A River Runs Through it.* [Film]. Burbank: Columbia Tri-Star. Based on the book, *A river runs through it and other stories by N. Maclean* (1976). Chicago: University of Chicago Press.

Rhodes, L. (1981). I had a cat: A language story. *Language Arts, 58,* 773–774.

Richardson, V., Casanova, U., Placier, P., & Guilfoyle, K. (1989). *School children at-risk.* London: The Falmer Press.

Rogers, C. (1956). What it means to become a person. In C. E. Moustakas (Ed.), *The self: Explorations in personal growth* (pp. 195–211). New York: Harper & Row.

Romano, T. (1994). Acts of passion. *Teacher Research, 2*(1), 41–52.

Rosenblatt, L. (1976). *Literature as exploration* (4th ed.). New York: Modern Language Association of America. (Original work published 1938)

Sarason, S. (1971). *The culture of the school and the problem of change.* Boston: Allyn & Bacon.

Schickendanz, J. (1990). *Adam's righting revolutions: One child's literacy development from infancy through grade one.* Portsmouth, NH: Heineman.

Schon, D. (1987). *The reflective practitioner.* New York: Basic Books.

Searls, E. (1985). Do you, like these teachers, value reading? *Reading Horizons, 25,* 233–238.

Shannon, P. (1989). *Broken promises: Reading instruction in twentieth-century America.* Branby, MA: Bergin & Garvey.

Shannon, P. (1990). *The struggle to continue: Progressive reading instruction in the United States.* Portsmouth, NH: Heineman.

Short, K. (1992). Intertextuality: Searching for patterns that connect. In C. Kinzer & D. Leu (Eds.), *Literacy research, theory and practice: Views from many perspectives, the forty-first Yearbook of the National Reading Conference* (pp. 187–198). Chicago: National Reading Conference.

Slobodkina, E. (1948). *Caps for sale.* New York: William R. Scott.

Smith, F. (1988). *Joining the literacy club: Further essays into education.* Portsmouth, NH: Heineman.

Smith, F. (1990). *To think.* New York: Teachers' College Press.

Spradley, J. (1980). *Participant observation.* New York: Holt, Rinehart & Winston.

Stevens, J. O. (1971). *Awareness: Exploring, experimenting, experiencing.* Moab, UT: Real People Press.

Sunstein, B. (1994). *Composing a culture: Inside a summer writing program with high school teachers.* Portsmouth, NH: Boynton/Cook.

Taylor, D. (1991). *Learning denied.* Portsmouth, NH: Heineman.

Taylor, D. (1993a). *From the child's point of view.* Portsmouth, NH: Heineman.

Taylor, D. (1993b). How do you spell *dream?* You learn—with the help of a teacher. *The Reading Teacher, 47*(1), 8–16.

Taylor, D., & Dorsey-Gaines, K. (1988). *Growing up literate: Learning from inner-city families.* Portsmouth, NH: Heineman.

Trelease, J. (1985). *The read-aloud handbook* (rev. ed.). New York: Penguin.

Van Manen, M. (1986). *The tone of teaching.* Ontario: Scholastic.

Vygotsky, L. (1978). *Mind in society The development of higher psychological processes* (M. Cole, V. John-Steiner, S. Scribner, & E. Souberman, Eds. & Trans.). Cambridge, MA: Harvard University Press.

Waller, W. (1932). *The sociology of teaching.* New York: Russell & Russell.

Wells, G. (1986). *The meaning makers: Children learning language and using language to learn.* Portsmouth, NH: Heineman.

Wells, G. (Ed.). (1994). *Changing schools from within: Creating communities of inquiry.* Portsmouth, NH: Heineman.

White, E. B. (1952). *Charlotte's web.* New York: Harper & Row.

Wilson, D. (1994). *Attempting change: Teachers moving from writing project to classroom practice.* Portsmouth, NH: Boynton/Cook.

Wilson, D., & Ritchie, J. (1994). Resistance, revision, and representation: Narrative in teacher education. *English Education 26*(3), 177–188.

Zen Buddhism: An introduction to Zen with stories, parables, and Koan riddles of the Zen masters. (1950). Mt. Vernon, NY: The Peter Pauper Press.

Index